TOUGHLOVE SOLUTIONS

The solutions presented in this book are what people have accomplished for themselves. Although we have concealed identities, these are *true stories* about real people who have been struggling to save their acting-out children and themselves from destruction. They report their stories in letters or by telephone to the TOUGHLOVE Network office or in person to us at TOUGHLOVE Weekend Workshops. For TOUGHLOVE is fundamentally self-help: people taking action for themselves, their families, and their communities; people working, sharing, and helping each other.

—the Authors

TIME MAGAZINE SAID OF THE **TOUGHLOVE** PROGRAM:

"An effective way of uniting parents to square off against the youngsters' own powerful peer group that endorses drug-taking and rebelliousness."

A SINGLE MOTHER WRITES:

"My TOUGHLOVE group helped me realize something about being a single parent: I love it. My whole family is happier now . . . It took some doing but I got over feeling abandoned and feeling sorry for my kids. I'm the parent now. I make the decisions and I know what's happening."

A TEENAGER WHO ATTEMPTED SUICIDE WRITES:

"My parents and all the other parents I have from TOUGHLOVE really turned my head around."

Bantam Books by Phyllis York, David York,
and Ted Wachtel

TOUGHLOVE
TOUGHLOVE SOLUTIONS

TOUGHLOVE
SOLUTIONS

Phyllis York, David York, and Ted Wachtel

BANTAM BOOKS
NEW YORK · TORONTO · LONDON · SYDNEY · AUCKLAND

*This edition contains the complete text
of the original hardcover edition.*
NOT ONE WORD HAS BEEN OMITTED.

TOUGHLOVE SOLUTIONS

*A Bantam Book / published by arrangement with
Doubleday*

PRINTING HISTORY
Doubleday edition published September 1984
Bantam edition / November 1985

*In this book, some names of TOUGHLOVE parents and their
kids, places, and identifying events have been changed.*

ISBN 0-553-27439-2

Published simultaneously in the United States and Canada

---

*Bantam Books are published by Bantam Books, a division of Bantam
Doubleday Dell Publishing Group, Inc. Its trademark, consisting of the
words "Bantam Books" and the portrayal of a rooster, is Registered in U.S.
Patent and Trademark Office and in other countries. Marca Registrada.
Bantam Books, 666 Fifth Avenue, New York, New York 10103.*

PRINTED IN THE UNITED STATES OF AMERICA

OPM   13 12 11 10 9 8 7

Contents

TOUGHLOVE SOLUTIONS

CHAPTER 1:

People Helping Themselves

TOUGHLOVE is a self-help program for troubled communities, families, and individual young people. Fostering a cooperative environment, the TOUGH-LOVE process enables people to take responsibility for meeting their own needs.

TOUGHLOVE establishes common ground. We adults have disagreed and argued. TOUGHLOVE looks for areas of agreement. For instance, we all agree that kids should not go to school stoned. Put aside all the explanations as to "why" they are stoned:

"School is boring."

"The curriculum is irrelevant."

"The teachers are just there for the money."

"Parents just don't care anymore."

"The kids today need more discipline."

"The whole world could blow up any day."

"My father never took me fishing."

"She had a tough time with our divorce."

1

The explanations can be infinite. TOUGHLOVE focuses on those matters in which we can find agreement.

TOUGHLOVE avoids blame. Blame keeps us helplessly trapped. Finding fault postpones dealing with the problem and ignores its broad base. Kids are in trouble everywhere in North America and they are from all kinds of families. Whom can we blame for a problem that is so pervasive?

TOUGHLOVE deals with the "here and now." Families in crisis don't have time to belabor the past. When the crisis eases, perhaps family history and patterns may be worth exploring. But when a young person is violent, untruthful, destructive, or irresponsible, the response needs to be immediate and in the present tense. Unacceptable behavior must stop. Beginning now.

TOUGHLOVE is action-oriented. The meeting structure we have suggested to parent and kid support groups builds in goal-setting and decision-making rather than bull-slinging and philosophizing. Time limits for each session of the meeting keep things moving.

Most of the action takes place between the meetings. People actively help one another achieve their week's goals. They call one another, they go to one another's homes, they house and talk with one another's kids, they give one another rides, they go to court or jail for one another. They don't just talk. They act by taking stands about behavior they are no longer willing to tolerate, by making weekly bottom lines for those small steps that will allow them to maintain their stand, and by developing plans about how they will manage to keep each bottom line.

TOUGHLOVE decentralizes authority. People in each community take responsibility for initiating a local parent or kid support group. There is no such thing as a TOUGHLOVE chapter. We issue no group charter and a group may not formally name their group with the registered trademark: TOUGHLOVE. There is no hierarchy or dues structure.

There is only the TOUGHLOVE Support Network, which maintains an informal listing of groups and publishes the quarterly *TOUGHLOVE Notes,* facilitating communication to and among support groups using the TOUGHLOVE philosophy. Troubled people who call and write the Network office are referred to groups in their area or assisted in starting their own community support groups.

Groups may use the TOUGHLOVE philosophy, the TOUGHLOVE self-help manual for kids, *TOUGHLOVE,* a book published by Doubleday and Bantam, attend the TOUGHLOVE Weekend Workshops, purchase TOUGHLOVE tapes, enroll members in the Support Network, or not. They may run their local parent support group without any affiliation with TOUGHLOVE whatsoever.

The groups in some areas have formed regional associations. Loosely organized, without bylaws or incorporation, representatives from area support groups meet monthly to exchange ideas, sponsor picnics, raise funds, and carry out public relations functions. Yet the associations have arisen without any official sanction, on the sole authority of people who wanted to improve relations among support groups.

TOUGHLOVE empowers people with skills and knowledge. Too often intimidated by experts, TOUGHLOVE participants assert themselves and demand involvement in decisions. They instigate action and collaborate with professionals, often achieving creative solutions and dramatic results that would otherwise have been unlikely or impossible.

Emphasizing cooperation, TOUGHLOVE avoids conflict. Through energetic public relations efforts, TOUGHLOVE support groups overcome resistance in their communities. People like judges, police officers, psychiatrists, psychologists, school personnel, social workers, or detention center staff are invited to attend TOUGHLOVE meetings. These visitors usually drop their negative stance and become TOUGHLOVE advocates when they recognize the cooperative spirit that prevails among TOUGHLOVE group members. In Bucks County, Pennsylvania, where TOUGHLOVE initially received a cool reception, a TOUGHLOVE mother was honored by Juvenile Court. She was presented with an award for her efforts to help kids in trouble and her cooperative attitude was acknowledged. No segment of the community can solve the problem alone: not the schools, not the police, not the courts, not the caseworkers, not the parents. We must all work together.

Finally, TOUGHLOVE encourages self-responsibility. There are no professional TOUGHLOVE organizers traveling around the continent starting parent support groups. Someone must take the initiative in each community to start and maintain one. If no one does, then nothing happens.

Thus the solutions presented in this book are what people have accomplished for themselves. Although we have altered names, places, or other facts to conceal identities, these are *true stories* about real people who have been struggling to save their acting-out children and themselves from destruction. They report their stories in letters or by telephone to the TOUGHLOVE Network office or in person to us at TOUGHLOVE Weekend Workshops or in our travels. For TOUGHLOVE is fundamentally self-help: people taking action for themselves, their families, and their communities; people working, sharing, and helping each other like the TOUGHLOVE group members in the next chapter, where we find a TOUGHLOVE group "checking in" with each other about last week's events.

CHAPTER 2:

Solutions

"He kept screaming and cursing at me and was so out of control that they handcuffed him and carried him out of the courtroom."

Mary cried as she spoke to the other parents in her TOUGHLOVE check-in group and the woman next to her touched her arm gently.

"But I know in my heart I did the right thing. As soon as the judge told him that he had to go to a drug rehab or face imprisonment, he knew that the TOUGHLOVE group had been involved behind the scenes. And that's when he started screaming at me. God, I'm glad Joan was there with me."

She smiled through her tears at the woman who had comforted her and all ten people in the circle burst into spontaneous applause.

"I know just how you were feeling," said a bald man opposite her. "The group supported us in pressing charges against our own kid. She didn't make a scene in the courtroom, but she wouldn't talk to us for weeks. We felt horrible."

His wife nodded, her face revealing the pain that the recollection held for her.

"But we stayed tough, thanks to everyone's help. Now she's going to the community college and holding down a full-time job."

His wife's face blossomed into a smile as she added, "And we have a daughter again. A real daughter who treats us like parents instead of like enemies."

Heads nodded around the circle, but one woman interjected, "Unfortunately, things didn't work so well with my daughter. After she ran away for the millionth time, I finally had the courage to refuse to take her home until she had a drug and alcohol evaluation. The counselor recommended a three-month stay at a rehab and she agreed to go. She lasted one week. We haven't heard from her since and that was almost two months ago."

Mary cringed. The woman continued.

"But the rest of my family is doing great. My husband and I are getting along and our sons are getting the attention they deserve. And there is no doubt in our minds how we will react when she returns. We'll send her to our TOUGHLOVE support family, the Ashleys. Our daughter can stay with them while she negotiates her way back into the rehab."

Joan touched Mary's arm again.

"She's right, Mary. You can't judge whether you did the right thing by your boy's choices. He may or may not straighten out his life. At least you've given him the chance. But what you did was right for the rest of your family, whether or not he changes the way you hope he will."

Mary nodded in agreement. "I know you're right. I just hope I can stick to my intentions."

"You will," said Joan, "and we'll be with you every step of the way."

There was a pause and then the man to Mary's left began speaking.

"Well, our bottom line for this week wasn't nearly as dramatic as Mary's. We said we were going to change roles this week. I agreed to deal with the kids and Jill was going to step back."

Jill sat next to him, grinning from ear to ear.

"How did it go, Jill?" a woman asked her.

"It was wonderful. Every time one of the kids asked me for something or tried to get into an argument, I just said, 'You'll have to talk to your father' and walked away. When I felt tempted to answer or argue, I went immediately to the telephone to call somebody in the group. I must have talked to Mildred twenty times the first two days, but it got easier after that."

"How was it for you, Roger?"

"Strange. Strange for me, strange for the kids. They keep asking, 'What's with Mom? What's wrong?' It's a nice change to see our kids wondering about us for once."

Suddenly a voice from the other side of the room interrupted. "Finish checking in. Large group in two minutes."

Jill and Roger indicated that they were finished checking in and the group turned to the next woman in the circle.

"I don't have much to report. My bottom line was the same as the week before. If Joey doesn't get home for dinner on time, he can't have any food."

"Is it working?" asked the bald man.

"Well, it has for almost three weeks. He's been home on time for dinner."

The other parents applauded.

"Who's your support?" asked Joan.

"Harriet. She called me every day last week at

dinnertime, but since it's been going good I told her I'd just call her if he didn't show."

Joan, as small-group leader, indicated to her circle of parents that it was time to join with the other parents in the room for the large-group session. Tonight the TOUGHLOVE group had invited representatives from the county juvenile detention center to observe the meeting and to discuss ways in which the parents and detention center staff could cooperate.

The parents in this room are looking for solutions. Realistic, practical solutions. Not theories, not reasons, not explanations. They are trying to stop their hurtful and abusive children from destroying themselves and others.

They no longer want to listen to a therapist who tells them that they are the cause of their child's behavior and if they can work out the problems in their relationship then maybe things will change. Or a youth worker who tells them their daughter's OK but they're just too uptight about marijuana. Or a school administrator who lectures them on getting their son to school when they've been driving him to the front entrance every day and he slips out the back.

They want solutions. Not blame. Not guilt. What, specifically, can they do to change things now? What will work?

Their children, young people from preteens to thirties, have created a dilemma for communities throughout North America. Stealing, lying, failing school, running away, vandalizing, harassing. Rude, drunk, drugged, lazy, violent. Their numbers in the United States and Canada have grown so rapidly since the sixties that the problem is pervasive. In cities, towns, and rural communities, there are schools where drugs can be purchased in the hallways and courts where lesser crimes are overlooked because there are so many felonies.

Not thousands but hundreds of thousands of families struggling with outrageous kids. And they need solutions. That's what brings them to TOUGH-LOVE. TOUGHLOVE offers solutions.

Solutions that are real, observable, and some-times dramatic. Kids actually changing. Getting bet-ter. Getting straight. Replacing abuse with consider-ation, neglect with concern, boredom with purpose-fulness, laziness with effort, drunkenness and drugs with sobriety.

Solutions not just for individual families but for whole communities. Like the TOUGHLOVE group in California that is raising money to establish an effective drug rehabilitation center. Or the joint proj-ect of eight TOUGHLOVE groups in Bucks County to initiate an alternative school to help kids change their negative behavior. Or the New Jersey group that provided the local high school with parent vol-unteers to help teachers monitor all-day study halls on weekends for teenagers who had been truant during the week.

When parents achieve solutions in their own families through cooperation with other parents, with schools, police, courts, and other local agencies, they begin to recognize the possibilities for solutions on a larger scale.

One of the most exciting solutions for helping troubled young people in the community is the grow-ing number of TOUGHLOVE groups for kids. Us-ing the structure and process of the adult TOUGH-LOVE groups, parents have begun to foster weekly meetings in which kids set bottom lines for personal change and support each other in accomplishing those changes.

Parents have even achieved "interstate" solutions

by using the TOUGHLOVE Parent Support Network (the coordinating organization for TOUGHLOVE located in Doylestown, Pennsylvania) to locate other TOUGHLOVE parents in distant places who could help them. A couple in Houston, Texas, for instance, were able to get parents to act as liaison with their son in jail in Hershey, Pennsylvania. After coming to terms with the young man, the stand-in parents arranged his release and put him on the bus for home.

What is especially interesting is that once parents begin to sense their own "personal power"—their own ability to make things happen—they begin to deal with other personal changes. Some parents become leaders when they have always been followers. Others stop smoking. Or stop drinking. Or lose weight. Or go to college. Or find the courage to bring a halt to physical abuse from a spouse or to end a horrible marriage by getting a divorce. Or recognize the need to "let go" of a child who wants to go out on his or her own.

TOUGHLOVE has begun to influence our society itself and its attitudes toward acting-out kids. Like the man who attended one of our weekend workshops and decided to stop using the euphemistic title of "school attendance consultant," which his up-to-date school district had bestowed upon him, and returned to the much clearer title of "truant officer." Or the therapists who are reexamining the blaming language and blaming stance they typically adopt in dealing with the parents of troublesome youth. Or the drug and alcohol addiction hospital which is establishing a treatment program for teenagers in coordination with TOUGHLOVE parents' and kids' groups in their area, based on TOUGHLOVE strategies.

Solutions. That's what TOUGHLOVE parent

support groups accomplish for families and communities. As 1981 opened, there were only a half-dozen groups in existence, limited to the Philadelphia area. But word gets around fast when something works well. The number of parent support groups in the United States and Canada using the TOUGHLOVE philosophy today is approaching one thousand.

"I'd like to summarize what we've just agreed upon before we go back to our small groups," said Marie, who had been heading up the large-group session. "First of all, we want to improve communication. Parents standing in for other TOUGHLOVE parents who have kids locked up in detention should call before they show up at the center. If any questions or problems arise, detention center staff should feel free to call Harriet, John, or me until we choose two members from our group to serve as the regular liaison. These two people will meet monthly with Art Clymer, the director of the center."

Both parents and detention staff nodded their heads in concurrence, reflecting the positive atmosphere in the room.

"OK. Anything else? All right then. Let's get back in small groups and set bottom lines for next week."

Joan's group formed a circle and she smiled at a blond woman next to Jill and Roger who had not spoken earlier.

"Sue, this is your second week with TOUGH-LOVE. Would you like to take a stand and set a bottom line this week? Last week you said you'd read the TOUGHLOVE parents' manual for this meeting, which I assume you did."

Sue nodded. "Yes, I did read the manual. It was really helpful because it described feelings and situations that I never expected to see in print. I even tried to get my husband to read it."

"Did he?" questioned Jill.

"No," Sue responded, almost bursting into tears. She paused and regained her composure. "He doesn't even want to talk about Billy. I think he's just so ashamed that he avoids the whole situation." Now she did burst into tears.

Jill stood up and moved her chair next to Sue's and put her arm around her.

"Sue, see that man over there?" Jill pointed at her husband, Roger, who was smiling sheepishly. "He and your husband must be identical twins because that's just how he was. He wouldn't read the manual, he wouldn't come to the meetings. Not until Harry Kline and Bob Marsh called him up and asked him if they could stop over to chat." She motioned in the direction of some men in the adjacent small group.

"I came to meetings for over a month before Joan and others persuaded me to set a bottom line to get my husband to the meetings. We set up a plan for other men to talk to him and Harry and Bob volunteered to be my supports."

"And I know how your husband feels," interjected Roger. "First of all, I always let Jill deal with the kids, like most fathers do, and secondly, I was immobilized by my shame. Harry and Bob put me on the spot by coming over to see me. But their candor was what really did the trick. If they could spill their guts about how horribly their own kids were behaving, then I felt less ashamed. So I agreed to come to a meeting and I haven't missed one since."

Sue looked very ambivalent.

"I don't know. I sort of like the idea, but I just don't know how he'd react."

"Maybe you just want to think about the idea until next week," Joan said. "Perhaps you want to try to take a stand and set a bottom line with Billy on your own this week, something small that will help build your confidence."

"Yes, I think I'll do that. I'd like to talk to Bill again, tell him about what happened at the meeting tonight, and maybe he'll come around that way. And in the meantime I might try something with Billy on my own. I've been thinking about some ideas since reading the manual."

"Great. What do you have in mind?"

"Well, I'd like to deal with Billy's rudeness and lack of consideration for others. I remember last week in the large group one of the parents made a presentation on dealing with behavior rather than drugs. In my situation I'm sure Billy's involved with marijuana, but I can't prove it. Like the man said last week—I don't have to prove it. I can just deal with what I can see. Like his sloppiness and his nastiness."

"Exactly," said Jill, still sitting next to her. "Boy, you learn fast. It took me a long time to get that through my head."

Sue smiled. "Well, thanks. But I'm not sure what to do next."

"That's what we're here for, Sue," said Joan. "The best way to develop a stand is to use an 'I will not' statement. From what you've just said, I'd suggest a stand like 'I will not accept rudeness and inconsideration from Billy anymore.' That would be your long-term goal, what you'll be working toward by setting weekly bottom lines."

"That sounds good. I think that's the stand I want. 'I will not accept rudeness and inconsideration from my son.' Then what do I do?"

The woman sitting next to Roger spoke up. "You need to pick something that really bugs you. I could tell you a million ways that my Joey is rude, but coming home late for dinner is the one I settled on for a bottom line a few weeks ago. I do all that work preparing a nice dinner and he would come home when the rest of us were having dessert—or later. Wow, that ticks me off. So that's where I've decided to start."

"Then I think I know where I want to start also. I can't stand his filthy room. I'm always picking up after him. You wouldn't believe how many wet towels, dirty clothes, and even dirty dishes I find in his room."

"Yes, we would believe you," Joan said with a chuckle. "That's a very popular beef among TOUGHLOVE parents. And dirty dishes in the bedroom are a good indication of marijuana use. Dope smokers usually get very hungry. The kids call it 'the munchies.'"

"Then Billy seems to have the munchies every night. What can I do about it?"

Jill responded. "You're not going to stop him from smoking dope easily. I'd suggest you focus on the dirty room issue that you just brought up. What you have to do is start acting different. That's the first step."

"Let's help her with some brainstorming," Joan suggested.

"Why don't you refuse to feed him if his room is messy, like I'm doing with Joey?"

"Lock his room until he promises to clean it," said Mary.

"Refuse to wash his clothes."

"Put all the dirty stuff in his bed."

"And then put his bed outside next to the trash cans," joked Roger.

The parents offered a rapid succession of ideas, some in jest. Some of the brainstorms that are offered as humor lead to creative and feasible actions. The brainstorming stopped after a couple of minutes and the group turned back to Sue.

"Do you like any of those ideas?"

"Well, I think I like the idea of putting all the dirty stuff in his bed. I just don't know if I can really do it. I'm afraid he might make a terrible scene."

Joan started to talk, but paused for a moment.

"You know, Sue, I think we're pushing you too far, too fast. Like Jill said, you seem to catch on to the ideas very fast. But knowing what to do and doing it are two different things. Maybe you should stick with the stand that you've taken, but make a much smaller bottom line. Like telling your husband what's happened tonight and what you're thinking about doing. See if you can get his support. If nothing else, you'll get him thinking about things. It sounds like you'll need his support if Billy makes a scene."

Sue seemed relieved.

"I think you're right. I'll take the stand that I won't accept Billy's rudeness and inconsideration. And I guess my bottom line is to tell my husband about the stand and what I might do as a bottom line."

"OK. Now you need a plan and support. The more specific you are, the better. Like, when are you going to tell your husband?"

"Tonight. When I get home."

"Good." Joan looked around the circle. "And who'll give her support?"

"I will," said Jill. "I'll call you to see how it went?"

"Fine," responded Sue. "Or if it's OK, could I call you tonight after I talk to him?"

Jill nodded firmly and touched Sue's arm. "You bet."

Everyone in the small group applauded and Joan asked who else wanted to work on setting a bottom line. All around the room, people were struggling with stands and bottom lines until Marie announced that it was time for the final session of the meeting. Parents formed into a large group again.

"OK. Let's go around the room quickly telling stands and bottom lines," said Marie. "Also, speak up if you need some support from other parents that you couldn't arrange in your small group."

"Right here. Alice Wendell has a meeting with the assistant principal at the high school on Thursday and no one in our group could make it."

"What time is the meeting?" someone asked from the other side of the room.

"Ten o'clock," answered Alice.

"I'll go to support you."

"Good," said the leader. "Talk to Alice after the meeting. Anyone else need some support? OK. Then let's hear those stands and bottom lines."

Each person who had taken a new step reported to the group and received a round of applause. Sue beamed as the group applauded her, obviously feeling encouraged by the events of the evening.

"OK. Sounds like we all did a lot of work tonight. Now I have an announcement. As most of you know, all of the human service agencies will be having booths at the Chestnut Mall this weekend. We'll be having one too. If you volunteered to man the booth, check with Ruth after the meeting to confirm your time slot. Any other business?"

"Yes, I'd like to say something if I may." Art Clymer, the director of the detention center, stood up.

"I just want to thank you for inviting us to your meeting. I know we've banged heads a few times in the past, but now I understand that you folks don't just kick your kids out of the house."

His comment was met by laughter and he continued.

"I'm looking forward to cooperating fully with your strategies. In fact, if it's all right with you, I'd like to have other members of my staff attend one of your meetings. I realize now why TOUGHLOVE has become so popular throughout the country and I'm excited by the possibilities. Best of luck to all of you."

The meeting ended with parents and detention center staff standing and applauding each other, for they all recognized that they had just taken an important step toward achieving solutions for the kids in trouble in their community.

CHAPTER 3:

Psychology as Part of the Problem

A young man who was convicted for a long string of burglaries was mandated to a drug and alcohol facility. There, in the family therapy session, he stated that the only reason he was in trouble was to keep his mother and father's marriage together.

A police officer reported that when he collared a boy who was shoplifting, the young fellow explained that he stole as a result of low self-esteem. He always had trouble in school, he said, because dyslexia kept him from reading.

A teacher told us of a student who claimed he couldn't do any schoolwork because he was an SED, a special education label which means "socially and emotionally disturbed."

In dealing with kids in trouble, psychology has become part of the problem. Reasons for outrageous behavior have become excuses for outrageous behavior.

"My dad was a drunk."

"I never got enough attention."

"I have a learning disability."

People do not have to be responsible for their actions when they can cite the reason that they're screwed up. We live in a society where a person's behavior is readily explained by "causes." Parental action or inaction can "cause" a child to behave a certain way. Therefore that child does not have to bear responsibility for his or her behavior.

Imagine the absurdity of a world where many people act like Geraldine, the comic character created by Flip Wilson. Raising hell until confronted, they say, "Well, don't blame me. The devil made me do it." Don't laugh. That absurd notion is contemporary reality among many professionals who work with kids in trouble. Every day young car thieves, vandals, burglars, and drug dealers are excused from real consequences of their crimes because they fit the popular psychological perceptions of the juvenile justice system. Every day some family therapists are telling parents that their relationship is the underlying cause of their child's unacceptable actions.

It is true, of course, that parents have a tremendous influence on their children. It is true, of course, that children are deeply affected by a father who molests them or a mother who abandons them. It is true, of course, that divorce can have a disruptive effect on a child's personal development. But ultimately we have to ask the question "Who's minding the store?" Who inhabits that human body and determines what it does? Who or what steers its course? Some external force? Parents? Past events?

Finding the "reasons" for behavior has become a cop-out. Kids have learned to use their labels to manipulate other people, even professionals, who are conned by smart youngsters who can "talk the talk." In an article in *The Family Therapy Networker*, R. D. Laing, an influential British psychiatrist, reported the following conversation with a teenage girl whose parents claimed she had anorexia. "The girl was very bright and knowledgeable about anorexia. She told me flat out, 'I'm not anorectic. I'm on a hunger strike against my parents.'" She may or may not have been knowledgeable about anorexia, but she sure knew how to get a psychiatrist to agree with her.

Like the boy with low self-esteem and dyslexia, or the SED student, or the kid who got in trouble to "keep his parents' marriage together," young people have grown up in a society attuned to psychological explanations. Psychology, psychiatry, therapy, and counseling have gained widespread legitimacy. Psychological testing is carried out routinely by schools, by the military, and by employers. Rival governments develop psychological profiles to evaluate the behavior of one another's leaders and advertisers scrutinize the psychological implications of their television commercials.

Specialties in psychology have proliferated. There are industrial psychologists, social psychologists, school psychologists, and child psychologists. There are sex therapists, marriage counselors, and drug and alcohol counselors. There are twelve thousand registered family therapists in the United States. There are peer counselors and horticultural therapists. There are even therapists for dogs.

Psychology is one of the favorite themes of mass media: from the daily funnies to Dr. Joyce Brothers, from Donahue to Dr. Quincy, we are deluged by psychology. Psychologists even host their own radio talk shows and sportscasters explore the psychology of the game in their locker room interviews.

But the mass media present shallow one-dimensional views of people and psychological issues. An episode of "Quincy," the crusading coroner of television, illustrates that medium's typical oversimplification of human behavior. A young man is murdered at a punk rock slam-dancing nightclub. The cause is the violent music, which exhorts young people to get stoned out of their gourds, punch, kick, and knock each other down. Quincy provides his weekly dose of righteous accusations against the week's villain. The characters are sketched with one-liners. Kids are hedonistic bums who tell Quincy, "Your generation screwed up the world and now you want us to fix it," while the single mother of one of the punk rockers is described as "too busy working to communicate with her daughter" by a psychiatrist who oozes professional concern from every pore.

Television programs explore issues in flat, quick, and cheap ways. Love becomes sex, sex becomes performance, anger becomes physical mutilation. Life takes on the qualities of a thirty-second commercial. Slogans and buzzwords take the place of complex events.

Like the word "communication." In the psychiatrist's quickie assessment of the working mom and her daughter, communication was lacking because they did not "sit down and talk." Didn't Mom communicate any love or concern for her child by working so hard? Are love and caring absent if mother and daughter don't sit down and talk about their problems?

Because most psychologists, therapists, and counselors do their job by sitting and talking to their clients, they see human relations in terms of their own world. A client is perceived to be improving when he or she is able to verbally communicate thoughts, feelings, and actions. The therapist is particularly pleased when clients can share how their relationship with their parents influences their present thoughts, feelings, and actions. Now they are *really* talking.

Communication in the form of sitting down and talking is thought not only to cure psychological problems, but it also is supposed to prevent them. This questionable assumption has its roots in Freud's Victorian cause-and-effect thinking: if the therapist identifies and removes the disease-creating organism, then he or she restores the human being to health. But if one catches the cause early, the assumption goes, one can avoid the problem completely. Supposedly, parents with children should sit down and talk a lot to avoid problems. Even better, parents should take "parenting courses," which teach folks how to talk with and listen to their children. Talking and listening is a process whose ultimate outcome is a discourse between equals, but kids in trouble have shown that they cannot manage equality.

Unfortunately, one-dimensional solutions do not work in a multidimensional world. Many well-meaning parents with outrageous kids have tried "sitting and talking" to no avail. How can you "sit and talk" with a druggie? How do you have a meaningful conversation with an altered consciousness?

Another psychological concept is that of "consistency." Parents should be consistent. Millions of heads nod in agreement. Wait a minute. How consistent can Mom and Dad be when they are just home from a tough day at work? Are angry with each other? Are getting divorced? Are worried about money, getting laid off, sick relatives, or their acting-out kid? When we're struggling with the inconsistencies of the world around us, consistency is often out of place.

For the therapist sitting in his office or institution, the setting is perfect for consistency. Every day, month after month, year after year, he counsels clients in the same environment, a stable pattern of existence and behavior which reinforces his emphasis on consistency.

If consistency means that parents should follow through on their discipline and not say yes when the other parent has said no, that seems simple enough. But does consistency mean always maintaining the same pattern? To the contrary, we feel that changing patterns—staying quiet if you are a yeller, yelling if you are quiet—that doing the unpredictable is often the best way for parents to deal with an acting-out kid.

Similarly, the psychological prescriptions of "openness" and "honesty" and "trust" may serve the therapeutic setting when people are acting in good faith, but maintaining these values does not help parents of destructive kids. In working with clients, the therapist establishes the rule of confidentiality. "What is said in this room stays in this room." For clients to share intimate and painful thoughts, there must be an environment of trust, a way of being together that leads many therapists to believe that the quality of the relationship is more curative than the content of the therapy. But that same trust and openness and honesty can make a parent or a therapist a patsy for a manipulative kid. Unless honesty is reciprocal, it will be disastrous. Trust and openness are the rewards for people who do what they say they will do. Trust is earned, it is not a birthright.

Once again the question "Who's minding the store?" How does a lack of communication justify a child's rudeness, stealing, lying, or running away? How can a person be excused from taking responsibility for his or her actions because of parental inconsistency? Psychology and psychiatry have done much to confuse the issue of personal responsibility.

A television show reported the tragic story of a sex offender who had several convictions for raping young children. During psychiatric treatment in a closed mental facility, the man became a model pris-

oner and even got married—with much fanfare—
while at the institution. Upon his release, he sexually
molested another child. The program included interviews with psychiatrists who stated that people
who commit sexual crimes suffer from a character
disorder which cannot be treated by current methods. If that is so, why did the psychiatric facility
accept, treat, and release the man? And who is responsible for his behavior?

Some courts are finding psychiatrists responsible. The family of a stabbing victim won a multi-
million-dollar settlement from a psychiatrist and institution that had treated and released the killer after
a previous offense, an identical fatal stabbing.

John Hinckley's attempt to assassinate President
Reagan raised the same issue. A battery of psychiatrists argued whether John Hinckley was responsible
for his actions or not. The jury said he wasn't. So the
injured parties are now suing his psychiatrist for
recommending that the Hinckleys not take their son
back home. The doctor believed that the tactic would
force John to take the responsibility for his own life.

Seeing all those psychiatrists contradict one another in the Hinckley trial cannot help but shake an
observer's confidence in the whole mental health
business. According to Dr. Loren Roth, professor of
psychiatry at the University of Pittsburgh, psychiatrists shouldn't be there. "Insanity is a legal issue and
not a medical concept; responsibility is a moral and
not a medical concept."

In fact, the American Psychiatric Association says
that courts should stop asking psychiatrists to testify
whether a defendant is sane or insane, responsible
or not responsible. Here again is a question of responsibility. Why don't the psychiatrists refuse to
testify instead of waiting for the courts to stop asking?

The issue of responsibility for behavior is critical

to behavior change. The therapists who assume that kids' parents are responsible for their teenagers' behavior are dramatically reducing the chances that the kids will change for the better. Why should they bother to change when the therapist has excused them and blamed their parents? Let Mom and Dad change. It's their fault.

Many therapists and counselors seem to lose their compassion for parents when they look at them through the lens of their favorite psychological theory or the eyes of a favored client. As parents struggle with the emotional upheaval in their lives, they need support and understanding, not blame. Guilt torments, it doesn't help.

A TOUGHLOVE group reported the following story about a bulimic daughter who had been away at college and was seeing a therapist weekly for counseling. When she came home for the summer, the therapist instructed her to eat by herself and *not join* her family during mealtimes.

During her first week at home, she spent one afternoon eating a five-pound roast, two pounds of potato salad, and an apple pie, the dinner which her mother had prepared for their large family. On another afternoon she ate a chicken and a chocolate cake, also the family's dinner. Her parents were quite upset and reported the events at their TOUGHLOVE meeting, where they were encouraged to call their daughter's therapist for advice.

They did.

"Why are you so involved in your daughter's eating?" was the therapist's first reaction. "You mean you *actually count food?*" came next.

Mom cried and Dad sputtered with rage. They ended the telephone conversation and called their TOUGHLOVE support people. Reeling with confusion and guilt, anger and doubt, they wondered if they were the "cause" of their daughter's problem.

Their TOUGHLOVE group set them straight. Helping them past their guilt, the group arranged an action plan. Their daughter would eat at a different TOUGHLOVE home each week. She would have her own refrigerator space and could prepare her own meals if she wanted to. Mom and Dad were relieved and their daughter seemed to enjoy working out the eating arrangements with other parents.

Because this plan was implemented at the time of this writing, the results are not yet in. But we don't have to wait to realize that the TOUGHLOVE group's approach was a great deal more compassionate to the family than that of the therapist. It also took the young bulimic out of her blame stance by removing her from the family. Since the therapist believed in "family systems" therapy, she presumed that the parents were interfering with the plan she had established for their daughter, an outcome the therapist had expected, since according to this concept the family needs a bulimic daughter to maintain the status quo. The bulimic focuses the parents' attention and energy, which prevents them from changing, and the parents' lack of changing keeps their daughter bulimic, a family dilemma to which only the therapist holds the key.

By thinking in terms of her set professional ideas, the therapist failed to appreciate the parents' human dilemma. The parents realized that they had been asked to back off, but it was impossible for them to do so when their kid was eating the family's whole supper. The TOUGHLOVE group's practical plan and support enabled the family to try a different solution, a solution that allowed them to disengage from their daughter's eating problem, while knowing she was safely provided for.

Are therapists villains? Of course not. Many therapists, counselors, psychologists, and psychiatrists have always encouraged parents to help their acting-out children take responsibility for their behavior, rather than dwelling on how parents might have caused that behavior. John Hinckley's psychiatrist encouraged his parents not to let their son continue to burden them with his irresponsibility by refusing to let him return home. The missing piece in that situation was alternative housing and support for their son that the TOUGHLOVE parents provide for one another's children.

We have received praise from professionals who feel that TOUGHLOVE groups are an aid to their own methods, providing a network of support for the parents they counsel. "When I urge parents who are involved with TOUGHLOVE to take difficult stands, like not letting their runaway come home without some commitments," one therapist told us at a conference, "I know that they have help available to them twenty-four hours a day from their fellow group members, a service I couldn't possibly provide."

Psychology and its related fields have the prestige of science in an age when scientists have become the new high priests of civilization. The twentieth century has dazzled us with scientific progress and dramatically altered our way of life. Yet, just as the miracle of nuclear energy presents the danger of nuclear war or reactor meltdown and the wonders of modern chemistry offer pollution and carcinogens, psychology has its dark side as well. Many of psychology's practitioners have followed a guru's trail, a practice that leads them to intellectualize human behavior into rigid cause-and-effect theories and leads them away from personal sensitivity. It is as if therapists are trying to fit into someone else's mold. Do people really maintain their family's status quo by keeping their kids sick? Nobody really knows because it's only a theory. But people do get frightened by their children's irresponsible actions, particularly when they are life-threatening, and that's a fact.

Psychology is an important discipline which holds out the promise of helping us to understand human behavior. But practitioners who operate from one-dimensional cause-and-effect assumptions which blame parents for their teenagers' behavior do not help anyone. Like "communication" or "consistency," cause-and-effect assumptions are shoddy oversimplifications which help destructive kids avoid the consequences of real life.

CHAPTER 4:

Families

"Dear TOUGHLOVE: We have raised six children. Four are now responsible adults in their late twenties and thirties. The last two are eighteen and twenty. They just lie around the house. When we speak to them, they ignore us or treat us with condescension. We don't understand them. We've never had these problems with our other children. Can you help us?"

" . . . I am a single parent and my ex backs up the children whenever I have problems with them, causing even more turmoil. My daughter seems to be fine at this point, but my son is having some beginning problems with dope. . . ."

". . . We just found out our fourteen-year-old daughter was involved in sex and that our sixteen-year-old son, a school athlete and honor student, has been taking drugs. We are heartsick. . . ."

". . . I am a divorced father and a single parent, as is my ex-wife. When we divorced, I was given custody of the children. We have maintained a good relationship and both work for the welfare of the children. Our fifteen-year-old daughter has just run away for the fourth time and we are beside ourselves. . . ."

". . . I am in that group of divorced mothers attempting to 'finish raising' their dear teenage children and I can use all the help I can get. . . ."

". . . We have a sixteen-year-old son who is not into drugs or alcohol but just thinks everyone should bow down to him. . . ."

". . . My teenage grandchildren are driving my daughter and son-in-law crazy. I wish there was some way I could help them, but everything is so different than when I raised children. . . ."

". . . As our kids got older, we decided to adopt two little boys. All was fine. We thought we had instilled all the fine qualities and principles into them that we had raised the others with. But things didn't work out that way. . . ."

". . . This is the second marriage for both my husband and I. We have his kids, my kids, and our kids. Our oldest is fourteen and has changed drastically in the last six months and I am ashamed of what's happening. I think it's time for some TOUGH-LOVE. . . ."

The concept and reality of family life have changed so drastically in recent years that we are struggling to cope with the new situation. We know that we are different than we once were, but we are not sure of the consequences.

We once stayed married "till death do us part." No longer. As many couples get divorced each year as get married. Half of our children are now "kids from broken homes." Part-time children living with part-time parents. Children of one family joined with the children of another family. This phenomenon has been reflected in the differences in television families over the years. When Archie Bunker's daughter got divorced, she was part of a trend leading to the single mother of "One Day at a Time" and the interracial single father and adopted children of "Diff'rent Strokes," both a far cry from "Ozzie and Harriet." Yet we pretend that these new families can cope and solve problems in the same way that two-parent families did in the fifties.

There is a new cynicism toward parents that dwells on the dark and seamy side of families. We have lost sight of the family as nurturing, affectionate, guiding, caring, supportive, and educative. Instead we focus on the family as violent, incestuous, abusive, controlling, and hurtful. We assume if something is wrong with a child that the parents did it, instead of seeing that most families are struggling with the same social changes that are buffeting us all about.

"Parenting" is a concept that has reduced raising children to a function. Parenting carries a kind of product orientation that sees the family as an assembly line, with parents manipulating different factors to produce a certain kind of kid. If parents could only perfect their technique, then they could turn out consistently wonderful children. When the kid is not wonderful, people assume that the parents goofed. They fail to recognize that challenges to our values and our life-styles also affect the way we bring up our children. Rather than criticize parents, we need to support them. We need to recognize that the problem is not parents themselves—but the new challenges facing them.

TOUGHLOVE is helping parents meet those challenges. The TOUGHLOVE support group creates an extended family that helps people deal with life's problems more effectively. TOUGHLOVE helps all kinds of families because all kinds of families are having problems with acting-out young people.

Remarriage creates a variety of family patterns which lead to new relationships between parents and kids. These new parent-child relationships, like all arrangements where one person is dependent on another, remain ambivalent. What is surprising is the intensity of these relationships. They are not cool, but burning with passion. Stepparents wanting desperately to be loved by their stepchildren. Biological parents feeling guilty about and protective of their children. Newly married couples struggling, as do all newly married couples, with retaining individual identities while forming a new union. Kids resenting the need to accommodate a new parent, even though they may like the person. The power battles are fierce under the best of circumstances, but they become completely unmanageable when a child's self-pity is reinforced by drugs and alcohol.

Sandy and her husband Elliot had divorced when Bennett was two years old. Elliot remarried soon after and saw Bennett only a few times a year. His new and growing family left him little emotional time and financial resources for Bennett.

Sandy managed to support Ben at first by cleaning houses. Later she opened her own cleaning service, took courses in bookkeeping and management, and became a successful businessperson.

Her parents helped her care for Ben. The family thrived. She and her son were close and depended on each other for nurturing. They had a special sense of togetherness that grew over the years.

When Ben was ten years old, Sandy fell in love with Don. Don made a concerted effort to get along with Ben and it paid off. Ben had a lot of respect for Don. After several years of indecision, Sandy and Don got married. Ben became more and more noncommunicative and secretive. By the time he was fifteen, his behavior had become so abusive that Sandy and Don came to one of our Weekend Workshops and Sandy told us her story.

"When Ben was fourteen, his grades dropped. He wouldn't go anywhere with us. When Don asked him to simply pick up a paper on the floor, he'd scream, 'Who the hell are you to tell me anything? You're not my father.'

"I could understand that he was jealous. After all, we'd been together so long until Don came along. But every time I tried to talk to him, he'd walk out.

"Then we tried not to say anything. We thought he was upset by our marriage and that it would pass, but he got worse and worse.

"One night he was brought home drunk by the local police. When I grounded him, he just walked out. Don told me he thought Ben was on drugs. But I said I never found anything. I was sure Don was wrong.

"One night Don confronted Ben about his drug use. Ben called Don every name in the book. He accused me of not loving him and of not trusting him. That night he didn't come home.

"Needless to say, things went from bad to worse. It's two years now since Don and I got married and I feel like we're on the verge of breaking up. I feel like I'm being torn in two. After all, Ben is my son. How can Don understand? I know Don loves me and has tried to be a father to Ben, but . . .

"Elliot took him back, but that only lasted three months and he shipped him back to us. Don didn't want to let him come back with us unless he sought counseling, but Ben refused and I let him come home anyway.

"Two weeks ago he was picked up for possession of drugs. He had pot and coke. He comes to trial in two weeks and I don't know what to do. I think my husband's right, but . . ."

In Sandy's story we heard all the pushes and pulls that stop her from acting to help Ben: the very special relationship they have had, her loyalty to him, her protection of him, all those years spent together. Sandy wondered, like so many other re-married parents we've known, "Maybe if I hadn't remarried, this wouldn't have happened" or "Maybe if my son and I weren't so alone and so close all those years, this wouldn't have happened."

Sandy feared the hand of a "stranger" on her boy, even though she loved Don very much. She was torn by her loyalty to her son that had developed over so many years. The balance of power in that special relationship had changed and Ben, who was both a child and his mother's equal, had become part of a threesome. Ben appeared to be fighting to dominate the new family, but in fact he just wanted to do whatever he wanted to do, while Don in some ways felt like he was in an inferior position to Ben.

As in most (but not all) relationships between stepparents and acting-out teenagers, it's the step-parent who recognizes the problem and the natural parent who hates to see it. But the stepparent cannot act without the backing of his or her spouse. TOUGH-LOVE groups help people like Sandy and Don get past this dilemma by giving the biological parent the support needed to back off and the new parent the support needed to get involved, not because there is individual or family pathology, but because these new families need support in managing difficult periods of change.

After the workshop Sandy and Don attended TOUGHLOVE meetings in their community. The group helped them go to court and let the judge know what was happening in Ben's life. The group supported them in seeking help for Ben through the courts and convinced Sandy to accept her husband's suggestion that they *not* hire a lawyer who might get him off the hook.

When Sandy and Don attended another workshop one year later, they told us that we had saved their marriage. Despite ups and downs, Ben was now living with his family again and things were working out.

Of course, we didn't save their marriage. Sandy and Don were willing to change the balance of power in their family. Sandy decided to be loyal to and protective of her son in a new way, to give up her exclusive relationship with him, and to risk letting the new father get involved with *her* kid. Don showed his caring by coming week after week to the parent support group, to counseling, and to court. Together they asserted their authority as parents and made Ben accept his appropriate role as their son and not their equal.

Accepting a stepparent into a family has the potential to create confusion, competing loyalties, and anger at a parent's new intimacy, at sharing a parent, at losing a parent. There are advantages to these new families as well. New marriages can bring more caring adults into young people's lives, an extended family with different opportunities for support. In some cases a new family provides an opportunity for distance from a natural parent who has been tough to get along with. A stepfamily is neither all good nor all bad. But when a kid is doing drugs, the process of adjustment becomes impossible. He or she has a lot to lose when a new stepparent enters the scene, sees things more objectively than the natural parent, and ends the old con game.

Typically, children manipulate their divorced parents, playing one off the other. Single parents frequently complain about their uncooperative spouse who backs up the kids whenever there is a conflict.

Or who doesn't get involved at all. An excerpt of a letter from a TOUGHLOVE parent illustrates:

> I am divorced, with two boys. There is very little interaction with their father and I cannot control them or what they do. They have been in a lot of trouble with the police and courts and I feel embarrassed and ashamed. I feel like a total failure as a mother.
>
> Many times I have wanted to tell the boys to shape up or ship out, but am more afraid of where they would go, how they would live, and what kind of horrible mother that would make me. I really need some answers.
>
> They have been rejected by their father many times and feel unloved by him. He says he loves them, but in the four years he's been gone, he has spent *very* little time with them, broken so many promises, and just left them feeling bad about themselves and unwanted by him. They love him, but cannot go to him for anything—all they get are excuses. I guess he loves them, but he's not a responsible person.
>
> I feel such guilt when I say, "That's it, I've had it" that I don't follow through and do much. I don't know what's good for them anymore, but I know living like they are is *not* good. I keep hoping they will outgrow this or see how bad it is for them, but I fear they won't.
>
> I guess I need to talk to others in my position and find out what will work for all of us in the long run. I love them so and just want them to grow up to be good men.

The dilemma is clear in this letter. Mom feels fear for her children's future, guilt about the past, and anger at her ex-husband. Her feelings keep her helpless to manage her kids right now and she needs to get some help. The solution rests with getting good information, developing an action plan, and securing support for carrying out the plan. That is what TOUGHLOVE has to offer.

My TOUGHLOVE group helped me real-ize something about being a single parent: I love it. My whole family is happier now. My two daughters, me, and my ex too (I guess). It took some doing, but I got over feeling abandoned and feeling sorry for my kids. I'm the parent now. I make the decisions and I know what's happening.

My kids are shaping up and they know they can't use anyone against me. I'm blushing when I say it, but I love being the boss.

Another single mom, Grace, had more than she could handle with her two sons, ages sixteen and seventeen. The last straw was when both boys were arrested for breaking into neighborhood homes. Grace, the judge, the probation officer, the school, and two TOUGHLOVE families worked out a plan. The boys had to attend school every day, make up their work, and pass each subject. The school agreed to report the results weekly to the probation officer. The boys had to work weekends for the TOUGH-LOVE parents and pay for the damaged and missing property from their burglaries. The TOUGHLOVE parents agreed to hire the boys to work around their homes. The boys understood that if they failed to live up to the arrangement, they would be remanded to the youth detention center pending a new hearing before the judge.

Many people can't imagine involving so many others in helping to manage their kids, much less getting assistance from acquaintances whom they have known only for a few weeks. One young girl told us, "My parents would have felt like failures if they had to do that." But that's exactly the point. TOUGH-LOVE parents *do* feel like failures before they get started with a group. Their situations are so desperate that being a failure doesn't matter anymore—they know they have to get things straightened out.

Then there is the "blended" family, with two parents and two sets of kids. The difficulties of living in a blended family are immense. Besides struggling with the new husband-wife and father-mother relationship, parents have to tangle with his kids-her kids issues plus new sibling rivalry. The situation requires the wisdom of Solomon, but most of us have only our very ordinary wisdom.

We live in times when we are urged to "express ourselves," a condition which leads some teenagers in blended families to vent their anger in ways that exceed the caring and nurturing available in the family. The new family can drown in its own chaos or its members can become solitary beings, avoiding interaction with anyone. Limits and boundaries are unclear and sorting out who is doing what to whom is difficult when acting-out behavior comes from all directions. Even worse is a situation where the kids unite to collude against their parents. Then parents are not only outmaneuvered, but outnumbered as well.

We have lots of blended families these days and they need a support system to help them learn and maintain coping skills. It takes a lot of work and a long time to achieve amicable peace in a blended family where acting-out behavior is prevalent. It's not like living with "The Brady Bunch." The involvement and cooperation of both adults is a necessity and good faith by each kid is essential.

The acceptance and prevalence of divorce means that relationships between husbands and wives are viewed as less permanent than relationships between parents and kids, leading us to focus on the kids and not the couple. Here is a couple, however, that decided they wanted more the second time around.

> After the workshop we realized that we have been trying to make a blended family out of the "bratty bunch," as you called them. Ellen and I have decided that our relationship has to come first. The kids will eventually leave home, but we want our marriage to last. We know we will work to raise the kids and do the best we can to help them through this angry time. Our fingers are crossed, but we're still holding each other's hand.
>
> Our TOUGHLOVE group is helping us to separate the wheat from the chaff and the chaos is slowly fading. We no longer ask the question "Who did it?" but instead we make it clear that we are all responsible for the fights and messes.
>
> (Sometimes I wish they would all go and live with our ex's.) Right now we're planning to go to school to find out what they have to say about our youngest kids. Thank God we have our support people to help us manage.
>
> Thanks again.

In some ways adoptive parents have a harder time with kids who get in trouble. They think things like "Maybe it's because I'm not the natural parent." They find it harder than biological parents to get angry. Biological parents may think or say, "I wish you were never born," but adoptive parents never say, "I don't know why the hell I ever got you," or "I wish you didn't have our name," or "I wonder whose genes you have." They must feel this way when their kids yell, "You only wanted me for yourself, not for me," or "You're not my real parents," or "We just don't mix. I'm different than you." At our Weekend Workshops we open up those issues and add a little humor so folks can admit to their anger without feeling they are being unloving.

After the San Francisco workshop I felt like I'd lost seventy-five pounds (not that I don't need to). When I went home and looked at my two *chosen ones,* the adopted brats, I really started laughing. I stood there thinking, "That's right, you two sorry sights. You better start to shape up if you want our *good* name." When Jerry turned around and said to me, "What the hell are you smiling at?" I just said, "At you two *orphans.*" I could see one nudge the other as I walked away. I felt so relieved of pity, pain, and sadness.

We know a family with six children (three boys, three girls) that they adopted through Catholic services. Three are now in college, one is finishing high school, one is in junior high, and the problem kid, Bobby, is locked up in a detention center. He is fifteen and has been raised, since he was five days old, in this loving, well-to-do, religious family. Like the other children, he was part of a large extended family whose grandparents, aunts, uncles, and cousins got together regularly for holidays and other family events.

By the time Bobby was ten, he was in a special class at school. Although he was bright, the school staff said he had "a behavior problem." The family went for counseling after Bobby started staying out later and later without permission and finally ran away.

By the time he was thirteen, he and his family

had spent two years in counseling. Just before age fourteen, he was admitted to a residential treatment program in a psychiatric hospital. After two months he was released and a few weeks later he stopped going to school, started staying out all night, and became verbally abusive to everyone at home. He was arrested for shoplifting, brought to juvenile court, and assigned a probation officer.

Now Bobby's parents were involved with a TOUGHLOVE group and realized that his arrest gave them more leverage. The next time he didn't come home at night, Dad called the probation officer and told him where Bobby might be. The probation officer picked him up and found him loaded on Quaaludes. He had ten more pills in his pocket. The probation officer took him to the local hospital for "detoxification," after which Bobby agreed to go into a residential drug treatment program rather than back into detention to await a new hearing.

At the rehab Bobby admitted to drug use since he was nine years old. From then on he felt there was something wrong with his family, that they were boring and behind the times. He couldn't relate to his father and felt that he was different and didn't need family. In his head he lived in a Peter Pan world without parents and without the need to ever grow up.

The family came to the rehab for six months for regular counseling sessions. Everyone—staff and family—was frustrated with Bobby because he still blamed and accused others, seldom looking at himself. After six months he was to be discharged and, although he said he didn't want to go home, he was certain that his family wanted him home.

His parents and brothers and sisters came to the last counseling session. Much to his surprise, they told him that they didn't want him home. All the family members told him that they had no more to give him and that if he wanted to be an orphan, that was his business. He would have to change his behavior and choose them if he wanted to be a part of their family.

Although he was shocked, he was also stubborn. True to form, he chose to go to a group home. His parents told him that they were there when he wanted to "adopt" them. At last report he had been kicked out of the group home for his outrageous behavior and was sitting in detention. His mom wrote recently:

> I am sorry about the life Bobby has chosen. All of us wish he had chosen our family and way of life.
>
> For so many years I felt I owed my children the best possible life. I guess parents feel that way automatically. I felt that our kids were a special gift to us since we couldn't have any of our own. I thought that God wanted me to take care of other people's children and give them good, decent lives. I still thank God for what He has given us.
>
> I feel bad that Bobby got in trouble at such a young age and that we didn't recognize the drugs. We kept thinking it was being adopted that really bothered him, especially since it troubled our other kids at one time or another. I tried really hard to be different for Bobby and give him more time. I think the whole family suffered because of all the effort I gave him, but I also think I learned that I can't make everything better.
>
> The last decision was a hard one, but the truth is I am too tired and so is everyone else. I felt guilt that maybe I was the wrong mother for

him, but I have stopped feeling that way since the other kids are so nice. I am sorry for Bobby, but I can't choose him. He has to want me. I hope someday he'll come home. Do you think I should send him a birthday card?

Her last sentence reveals her inner emotional struggle. TOUGHLOVE is probably tougher on her than it is on her son. She understands intellectually that she has to back off from Bobby, but she still yearns to be his loving mother.

Other parents get caught by viewing their children as victims. This is particularly true for well-intentioned people who adopt children of different races.

My husband and I have been married for twenty-nine years and have five children. Our two youngest children are adopted American Indians. Our older kids have grown up well, but our two adopted kids have been nothing but trouble.

We know we have been too soft with them. They have stolen from us and our neighbors (almost $8,000 worth), but we feel they have special problems, being adopted and being Indian. If we had pressed charges for the car stealing and check forging, they would be in reform school now. My husband and I would hate to see that happen.

Our bishop and a counselor suggested you might help us.

Years ago we didn't tell our children that they were adopted. We kept it a secret. Some kids found out and were greatly hurt. Others had to be told because they had physical maladies of genetic origin. But many of these adopted kids still have no idea that they are not the biological offspring of their parents.

Today almost every parent tells children at an early age that they were adopted. The children grow up with that knowledge and often begin to ponder the issue as they mature. They wonder, "How come my real parents didn't want me?" Given our preoccupation with "the individual," there is a great value placed on searching out one's natural parents. Television programs dramatize the issue and usually show happy endings where the biological parent and child are reunited, achieving peace at last! Adoptive parents want what's best for their kids and many have given their permission and help to their youngsters to seek out their biological parents. They do so even though they are fearful about what will happen, even though their hearts say, "Want and appreciate me. I don't want to share your love. Aren't we enough?"

Dolores was seventeen when her parents joined TOUGHLOVE. She was an adopted child, having lived with her folks since infancy. But for two years she had been doing poorly in school, smoking dope and drinking, hanging out with older guys, and staying out all night with increasing frequency. She wouldn't go to counseling, despite her parents' pleas, and she knew that her parents' threats faded away whenever she came home. That is, until her parents greeted her at the door one Sunday morning as she returned from another overnight adventure.

"We didn't think you wanted to live with us anymore so we packed your things." They handed her a paper bag full of clothes with a teddy bear perched on top. "We've made arrangements for you to stay with someone else until you decide what you want to do." They gave her a slip of paper with a name, address, and telephone number on it and shut the door in her face.

Dolores flew into a righteous rage, pounded on the locked door, and cursed at her parents. "I'll get my birth certificate and find my real mother," she screamed.

She hitchhiked to her boyfriend's house, but his father turned her away. He said he was tired of her staying there and that he didn't want legal responsibility for her. She muttered something about her parents not wanting her anymore, but then quieted down. She began to suspect that her parents had called him, especially when he offered to let her use the telephone. She didn't know where to go next, so she called the number on the paper.

The woman who answered invited her to come over and talk, but when Dolores asked how she should get there, the woman asked her how she got to where she was.

"I hitchhiked," Dolores responded.

"Fine. Then you can hitchhike here," the woman said as she hung up the phone.

"This is crazy," Dolores muttered. "Doesn't she know hitchhiking is dangerous?" Her boyfriend's father overheard her ironic comment and offered to give her a ride. On the way she made another attempt to con him with her adoption story, how her parents didn't really love her and how she was going to find her real parents. He didn't respond.

The woman greeted her at the door and let Dolores talk a while. She ignored the comments about her adoptive status and explained the conditions for her return home: no going out for a week, coming home directly after school, and arranging for regular counseling. Staying out overnight was absolutely unacceptable and would result in ejection from her home again. Dolores said she wanted to think about it.

That evening Dolores met the other members of the family, except one son who was away at college. He had been a druggie and was the reason this family had joined TOUGHLOVE. But his older brother had graduated from college and lived at home. She was very impressed with him and they chatted in the living room after dinner.

She started telling him her troubles with her parents, but when she mentioned her adoption he interjected, "Oh, you're adopted. Then I guess you owe them a lot for all they gave you." She was surprised by his remark and had never thought about being adopted in those terms. She admitted that she sometimes thought they were jerks for taking all her crap.

"Oh, you're not so bad that you can't change things," he said. "You can earn their love."

She pondered his comment all night and by morning had decided to agree to the conditions for her return home. When she and the TOUGHLOVE family got together with her family to discuss the arrangements for her return, she asked how she could earn their love, which surprised everyone.

Her father responded with tears in his eyes, "By adopting us." Her mother agreed. And two months later, when she had proved her intentions by changing her behavior, she did just that. In a ceremony at a TOUGHLOVE meeting, Dolores gave her parents a certificate of adoption that she had made and they gave her a birth certificate.

"It was a little embarrassing," she said later, "but necessary. I've decided to wait till I'm older to find my other parents—if ever."

We can continue to discuss the merits of telling kids they're adopted or not and encouraging them to find their biological parents or not. But whichever approach one takes, it has little or nothing to do with how to deal with the kids who bring us to TOUGH-LOVE. For they will always exploit the issue of adoption to justify their lack of consideration and their unkindnesses toward their adoptive parents.

We receive inquiries from parents who are having troubles with their young children. We respond by explaining that TOUGHLOVE does *not* deal with child-rearing. Rather, it deals with family crisis caused by young people who are literally out of control with dope, booze, and outrageous behavior. Yet we have come to realize that TOUGHLOVE does have some important implications for young families struggling with behavior problems. Coming for help with an older child often leads to dramatic changes for the whole family.

Facing the same cultural challenges as TOUGH-LOVE parents, young parents need support. Traditionally, support came from their extended family, but for today's mobile nuclear family that kind of support is often too far away. Furthermore, once young folks are having trouble with their kids, whether they live near their relatives or not, they may need some structured support which can help them *make changes*.

A couple came to a therapist we know on the recommendation of their son's school guidance counselor. Their eldest had started failing in school and was caught with several joints in his possession. The mother was a full-time housewife and mother who worked hard at both and had taken parenting courses to improve her skills. Her husband worked two evenings each week, in addition to his daytime job, because he felt it was important to provide for his family as best he could.

Our counselor friend assessed the family situation: besides their fourteen-year-old son, their ten-year-old daughter was acting sexually precocious, their eleven-year-old was smoking cigarettes, not doing homework or helping around the house, and their four-year-old complained that the ten- and eleven-year-olds hit her all the time. The parents themselves were overwhelmed. They believed that something was wrong with them or the home life they were providing. They felt that what was necessary was more love, more forgiveness, and more freedom. They didn't believe in punishment or spanking, but thought that reasoning, explaining, and understanding would solve their problems.

The therapist recommended that the parents join a TOUGHLOVE group for their older son and work with him simultaneously around issues with the younger kids. They agreed and he took them to their first meeting. He knew that they would need a lot of support to regain control of their family, for their children saw them as people who couldn't stop them. The family and the TOUGHLOVE group worked out a plan to have the older boy evaluated for drug and alcohol problems. The young man agreed to visit the outpatient clinic for three months. He received tutoring from another TOUGHLOVE mom in math, his worst subject.

After several weeks of therapy sessions, with the younger children making their demands and the parents expressing their frustrations, an incident occurred which gave clarity and direction to the chaos. Ten-year-old Jane was insisting on going roller skating with a twelve-year-old girlfriend, while her parents kept explaining that her friend was older and interested in boys and that they felt Jane was too young to get involved with boys. They were afraid, didn't want her to go, and explained again and again that she was too young. Jane persisted in her demands, saying that she was old enough and that she wasn't afraid.

Eventually, the therapist intervened, out of his own frustration with their endless argument, saying forcefully, "Jane, you can be a little kid. You can stay home and have stories read to you by your parents just like Marianne." She suddenly fell quiet.

The father, seeing the therapist's impact on his ten-year-old daughter, turned to his eleven-year-old son and stated firmly, "And you're just a kid, too. You won't be doing any more smoking and we'll start working on your homework." The boy sensed his father's resolve and stayed quiet.

The therapist, the parents, and the TOUGH-LOVE group planned some strategies for managing the kids. Both parents were surprised that the kids let them take charge again and that they actually seemed thankful for their parents' protection, although at times they were resentful. Overall, the situation improved dramatically.

Trapped by their own version of the American Dream, these folks were not "bad parents." They were parents who had lost authority in their own family because they didn't want to be authoritarian. Relying on the notion that love and understanding will take care of everything, they found themselves surrounded by their children's destructive behavior. They had lost sight of the fact that their kids needed the security of their authority around issues they were not ready to handle. With the therapist's corrective information and with the support of the other TOUGHLOVE parents, they were able to turn the situation around and enforce more age-appropriate behavior with their kids.

We also receive many inquiries from relatives. Concerned grandmas, worried brothers, helpful aunts, loving sisters-in-law, all wondering if TOUGHLOVE might not be helpful to their loved ones, people in their family. But they are often timid in their request.

> My sister has a daughter who is fifteen and a half. She has left home several times. Who she lives with, we don't know. She comes home, she says, because she's hungry. She is on some kind of drugs. When she's home, she doesn't do anything but eat and sleep. She is supposed to be at school, but she doesn't go. My sister doesn't know what to do, so she doesn't do anything. Should I stay out of this or try to help?

The author of this letter sounds like she feels she might be meddling. Our response: get involved. Try to help. Don't hesitate for a moment. If you love your sister and your niece, you have every reason to try.

We all get stuck, in one way or another, at one time or another. Though we don't always ask for the help, we often appreciate someone trying. Even if it doesn't solve the problem, it makes us feel good to know that someone cares.

The author of this letter might take her sister to a TOUGHLOVE meeting. Many folks, particularly single parents, come with friends or relatives to TOUGHLOVE meetings. Some parents bring their mothers or fathers or boyfriends or older kids or anyone who might help them carry out their weekly bottom lines. Some parents bring their relatives who are siding with the kid, so they can understand what TOUGHLOVE is all about and help, instead of hinder.

Grandparents have unique problems in today's society. For instance, they often find themselves cut off from their grandchildren when their own children get divorced from their mates. They have no custody rights defined by law, so there have been instances in which grandparents have sued for visitation privileges.

Similarly, grandparents often see their young grandchildren suffering from the abuses of their own sons or daughters. But they need not feel totally helpless because there are some things that they can do.

When our daughter, Beth, was sixteen, she had a baby boy out of wedlock. My wife and I took her and the baby in. Beth is a drug addict and has been in a lot of trouble. She has been in two drug programs. She gets better, then starts up again.

Beth is twenty now. Last year, when she got out of the drug program, she took Steven to live with her. We miss him very much, since we have been raising him, but she is the mother.

Things went OK for a while. We saw them every week and we often baby-sat for him. But soon Beth began picking him up late and then one time she didn't come back for two days. She was getting into her old ways, but when we offered to take Steven back, she got furious. She said we were accusing her of being a bad mother and we didn't see them for a while.

A couple of months later we got a call from our daughter's neighbor, who told us that Steven was being left alone a lot and that he cried a lot. We went to her house. She was there and we asked if we could take Steven out. He was dirty and skinny and very happy to see us. Her apartment was a mess and her television was gone. A disgusting man was living there with her. We wanted to ask if we could take Steven home with us, but we were afraid she'd get angry again and not let us visit with him, so we kept quiet. We took him out and bought him dinner and some clothing.

Thanks to God we saw you on television the next day and we called about a TOUGHLOVE group in our area. We started going to meetings and we still do.

First we got really good advice which we used. We reported our daughter to her probation officer. We had been afraid to do it, but with the group's help we told her about our daughter's drugs and she may put her in another program.

We also reported our daughter to Child Welfare and told them that we would be glad to take custody of Steven. Our friend Louise, who is in our TOUGHLOVE group, came with us and told the social worker how we had been going to the meetings and what we had been doing to try to help.

We told my daughter what we had done. She screamed and yelled at me and my wife. But she sent her boyfriend away. I guess she didn't want Child Welfare to see him there.

We wrote a letter to Child Welfare explaining everything that happened and why we wanted custody of Steven. We told them that maybe she needed a longer program and that if she was a fit parent we would gladly give up Steven to her. We still don't know what's going to happen in the long run, but we have temporary custody of Steven.

We still go to TOUGHLOVE meetings every week. We have made a lot of new friends and we are able to help other people now. TOUGHLOVE is a wonderful idea. Thank you for inventing it.

So many grandparents are stuck in a tough situation. They may have to let their children do what they want because they're out on their own, but loving their grandchildren, they worry about their welfare. In fact, their kids may actually blackmail them, knowing that they want access to their grandchildren.

Celia and Max, a couple in their fifties, have a daughter, Susan, who had been in and out of trouble since her teens. Finally, she seemed to settle down. She married a recovering addict, David, and they had two little girls. But Celia and Max were always bailing them out of financial problems. They paid for clothing and nursery school for the girls and sometimes paid rent and car payments. There was always some reason that their son-in-law was out of work: layoffs, unappreciative bosses, illness. The grandchildren always looked like ragamuffins, even though they had decent clothes.

One day Susan called them hysterically, asking them to come and get her and the girls. David had beaten her up. But in a few days they had reconciled and she went back to him. It was then that Celia and Max joined TOUGHLOVE.

Several months later a new crisis arose. Their son-in-law lost his job and the family couldn't stay in the apartment. Susan asked if her family could stay with Celia and Max for a week or two until things got settled. She said she had a job opportunity and when David got his first unemployment check they would get another apartment. Against the advice of their TOUGHLOVE group, Celia and Max agreed, saying things like "Where would the babies go?" and "It's only for a short stay."

The visit was intolerable. Susan and David didn't get up when the girls cried in the morning, knowing full well that Celia would attend to them. They didn't clean up after themselves. They let clothes pile up anywhere and reused them when they ran out of clean clothes. Celia and Max were disgusted and told the TOUGHLOVE group so. With support from the group members, they confronted their daughter and told her their complaints. The situation improved somewhat for the rest of their stay.

But once again when Susan and David found an apartment, Celia and Max paid the rent and deposit, filled the refrigerator with food, and supplied some new furniture. They simply wanted to help the kids off to a fresh start, but were unwittingly supporting irresponsible behavior. When they reported back to their TOUGHLOVE group, their friends teased them about what softies they were.

Three months later Celia and Max got another emergency call from Susan. She and David had to leave the apartment and needed a place to stay. That was the last straw. Max told Susan she couldn't come back, that he was sick of "saving her ass," and that if she wanted to communicate with them she could do so through another TOUGHLOVE parent. Celia gave her the phone number and hung up the receiver. They looked at each other, hugged, and cried.

In tears, Susan called their TOUGHLOVE contact, Marsha. "How could my parents do this to me?" Marsha explained that they couldn't stand seeing her ruin her life and that until she and her husband demonstrated some responsibility, Celia and Max didn't want to see them.

"We can make it without them," Susan declared angrily.

"Your parents will be OK with that," responded Marsha.

In the next few months Celia and Max carefully avoided contact with their daughter. They desperately wanted to call or visit the babies, but they knew they always had fallen for that hook. No more black-mail. When they felt tempted, they called or visited someone in the group.

They received cards in the mail: Max's birthday, Mother's Day, Father's Day. They missed Susan, but they especially missed their granddaughters, who were innocents in the whole matter.

Celia and Max heard through the family grape-vine that Susan was working hard and David was going to counseling, working part-time, and watch-ing the kids. Celia told Max excitedly, hoping that he'd agree that they should call the kids, but they both realized that would be a mistake. Instead they called Marsha and asked her advice. She called Su-san, checked out the situation, and called them back.

"I'm going to pick up your granddaughters on Saturday morning and I'll take them back Sunday night," said Marsha.

Celia and Max were thrilled.

"But one condition," said Marsha.

"What's that?" asked Max.

"You may only buy them one toy each and noth-ing else. No clothing, nothing else. Their parents have to take that responsibility."

"It's a deal!" shouted Celia, knowing that she would have a tough time resisting the temptation to shower the little ones with gifts.

Celia and Max see their grandchildren regularly now, picking them up themselves but not going in the apartment. Susan and David have a long way to go, but they're doing better. Other members of Celia and Max's extended family think they're horrible for limiting their relationship with their daughter and son-in-law, but the TOUGHLOVE group meetings help them stick to their resolve. They have a place to air their feelings and people to help when they need it. And they enjoy helping others.

No panaceas. Nobody gets to ride off into the sunset happily ever after. But a workable solution for grandparents who have trouble saying no, but must. For the sake of their daughter and her family, they have to keep on saying no.

We also need workable solutions for other problems. With divorce rates of 50 percent and higher in some places and with the prevalence of drug and alcohol abuse among young folks, single parents especially need support in raising their children.

I am writing to you because I may need your help. I live in an affluent suburb that used to be the All-American neighborhood. When my family moved into our split-level dream home eleven years ago, almost everyone around us had a two-car, two-parent, two-kid family.

But a strange thing has happened since then. Half of the two-parent families now have one parent. In fact, I recently realized that I'm the *only* daddy left on our block. My wife and I have been hearing a lot from our neighbors about their difficulties with their kids. Many moms seem ready to tear their hair out.

Last week my son and his friend were swimming in our pool, horsing around. I asked them to stop. My son stopped, but this other boy, who I have known since he was two, just continues and ignores me. I went into the house, put on my suit, ran back out, dived in the pool, and grabbed him. At first he thinks I'm kidding, but when I heave him out of the pool, he's shocked. I said to him, "Listen up. When I tell you something, I don't want you to ignore me." I go on about how long we've known each other and how respect is something we've got to have for one another. He really seemed to listen and he apologized.

Well, that night I got thinking and I came up with an idea that I've been kicking around with my wife and friends for a couple of weeks. I'm the only dad on the block, so maybe I could act as dad to some other kids besides my own. My wife organized a meeting of the moms on our block for Friday night and if it goes well, we'll expand to other blocks in the development. I'm sure that other dads would be willing to help.

I'm not sure exactly what we're doing, but I thought maybe we might start a TOUGHLOVE group. Please send me some information and any advice you might offer.

New structures for new situations. If we face our problems with creativity and a willingness to experiment, we can meet the challenges of our changing times. But even our new solutions must be sensitive to the exceptions, to the situations that don't fit the new solutions. By avoiding rigidity, we will respond flexibly to individual needs.

A couple of years ago we met a young woman, Janet, whose parents belonged to a TOUGHLOVE group near us. Janet was their oldest child and when she became a teenager she began to demand more freedom than her family was willing to give. Her parents were good people, active in their community, with strong church interests and a caring extended family. The family had strict rules, definite curfews and chores, and somewhat "old-fashioned" ideas about dating and teenage social life.

Janet seized her freedom. She began to sneak out to see guys, stay out all night, and cut classes at school. She found her way into the drug scene and was away from home for longer and longer periods. Her parents reported her as a runaway, but little happened until she was arrested for shoplifting at about the time her folks joined TOUGHLOVE. A smart judge let her choose between drug rehabilitation and detention.

Janet chose treatment. She did very well and her family attended weekly counseling sessions at the rehab. They worked through lots of hurt and pain. Janet began to visit home on weekends, avoiding her old druggie friends. As her discharge plans were made, old conflicts began to surface. The parents wanted her home under their old rules: ten o'clock curfew on weekends, all meals eaten together, and so on. Janet expressed her frustration, saying that she didn't know if she could abide by their rules. They all struggled for a compromise but were worlds apart in their values, even with Janet behaving responsibly.

The parents talked to other folks in their TOUGHLOVE group. Some parents suggested that they hold out for their own values, insisting that Janet return home on their terms. Other parents, who felt her family was too strict, urged Janet's parents to back off and change some of their demands. But finally the group began to realize that either position forced Janet or her parents to make concessions that neither was really willing to make. Furthermore, Janet's parents had other children in the household who would expect the same treatment as Janet when they got older, an awfully big change for the parents to accept.

Then someone suggested a new path: perhaps Janet's parents would have to allow their daughter to live elsewhere, as if she had grown up and moved out on her own. Although they weren't sure, Janet's folks agreed to pursue that possibility. More than anything, they wanted to keep their relationship with the daughter they loved without abandoning everything they believed in.

The situation was resolved with Janet living in a foster home for a year, finishing high school, and working part-time to earn money for college. She visited her family, but the relationship was superficial. Nonetheless, it fulfilled some emotional needs for everyone concerned.

Janet developed healthy relationships with a couple of women teachers at a community college who took an interest in her. Sometimes she slipped back into her drug abuse, but she always managed to find a kind heart at the college who got her to an Alcoholics or Narcotics Anonymous meeting and helped support her emotionally when she felt lonely. She continued to visit her family, but showed them only her strengths. Her problems and weaknesses were played out with her friends at college. She graduated from community college and now lives with a girlfriend and her mom. She seems to be doing fine.

For whatever reason, Janet defined herself outside of her family. She doesn't like her family very much. She says that they're too rigid. She loves them, but she can't stand to be with them for very long.

Although most of us want to see families that live happily ever after, that's not realistic. Whether or not we like her solution, it worked for Janet and her family. Forcing Janet to return home might have sent her back to her old behavior, but with a flexible solution, Janet and her family were able to maintain their relationship as Janet made her own way in the world. The purpose of TOUGHLOVE is to help families find limits and boundaries within a dramatically changed society and narrow thinking will not help.

Our culture is now creating a new set of expectations for parents. Dads are supposed to be more physically nurturing and moms more into their work outside the home. These new expectations will produce both good and bad outcomes. Some kids will slip between the cracks as parents struggle to sort out their roles. Grandparents may have ambivalent feelings about these changing roles, criticizing daughters or daughters-in-law who don't want to stay home with the kids or sons and sons-in-law who seem more concerned about their child's development than advancing their careers.

What about kids growing up in these different families? Identity and power won't be derived from being male or female, but how will it be acquired? Will nurturing dads be more effective disciplinarians with their children? Perhaps the nature of the oedipal conflict will change and kids won't have to push their folks away so hard.

The family is a dynamic system and responds to cultural influences and expectations. These changes will have both positive and negative effects and will require new outlooks and responses. Whatever happens, we believe that families need a supportive community to work through the unexpected and hurtful aspects of change, so that our children grow up well.

CHAPTER 5:

Runaways

When we hear about teenage runaways, we think of harsh families filled with drunkenness and poverty, physical and sexual abuse, and parents who don't want their children. We think of teenagers forced into prostitution, drugs, crime, and early death, kids who are victims of their uncaring and hurtful parents. These are the *Throwaway Children* that Lisa Ricchetes wrote about in her well-known book. They are kids who come from mean homes, kids who need to be mean to survive on cold city streets, kids who out of desperation choose desperate lives.

Many of these young people run away from harsh environments to a fantasy of glamour, adventure, and freedom. Young women dream of seducing, managing, and being chased by men, of being cared for, paid for, and wanted because of their beauty and power. They have visions of themselves as temptresses, seductresses, and kept women. Young men have a similar fantasy, of being cared for, of owning and being owned, of being handsome, ruthless pimps with kept women who want to be part of their stable falling all over them. Young male and female runaways maintain and are sustained by a drug-oriented hustlers' world, a life-style based on selling the only available product, their bodies. They end up, not with their fantasies, but in the dirt of the streets as pimps, whores, druggies, winos, thieves, hustlers, and corpses.

These are the images that haunt us all. But there are other kids out there, not running away from something, but running to something. Something they call partying. They come from families that care about them, from loving homes: wealthy, middle-class, and poor of every race. Like the cab driver in Mississippi who told us, "I jus' don' know. My daughter says she don' believe in Jesus no more and she's jus' runnin' wild. The wife and I are near goin' crazy." And the film executive in California: "I'm desperate. My kid comes and goes. We've gone the route: psychiatrist, counselors, special schools. Nothing seems to help. His friends all look like bums and he fits in with them like a glove. We're scared to death of how he'll end up." Families who fear the dangers of their kids' choices, while their kids see only the excitement and fun. Kids who are busy partying, doing dope, skipping school, shoplifting, hitchhiking, screwing around, and making believe they are adults.

We call these young folks "run-tos" because they are running *to* partying and *to* where they get the least hassle. When the streets get tough they come home, when home becomes a bother they leave. They represent three quarters of the estimated million or more kids who run away each year. Like the boy who wrote us that "I just got tired of being poor and told what to do so I left" or the girl whose mother said, "My daughter lives with her father in California, her friends down the street, and God knows where in between."

A run-to stays around the neighborhood or takes to the road, often phoning home to ask for something. The run-to has a network of resources and can find a place to stay almost any night. He or she will stay overnight with friends' families or relatives, a couple of days with young people who have their own place, a three-day stay with a girlfriend's or boyfriend's family, or an indefinite stay with a more lenient family or Good Samaritan. Run-tos represent themselves as polite, nice kids who have troubles at home, a pop psychological view we are all too eager to accept. In television, magazine, and newspaper stories about runaways, whatever the kids say is reported as fact without considering that they may lie or distort for their own purposes.

"You know how I managed to stay out on the street?" one young man boasted to us. "I just told everybody my stepdad beat me and there wasn't any place for me. I got so good at it I could make myself cry."

The media thrive on sensationalism, the stuff that sells, so all kids become victims and all parents ogres, a neat package that doesn't ask us to do anything but feel sorry for the kid, put blame on the parents, and say, "Ain't it awful." But kids stay out because staying out is easy and as long as it stays easy the run-to stays out. Eventually, the run-to gets tired or runs into too much hassle and heads back home.

"I came home," said seventeen-year-old Laurel, "because it was too hard on the street. I ran out of money and my friend's folks asked me to leave."

Run-tos can also develop dangerous and unhealthy life-styles. They hang out with sleazy people, steal for income, trade sex for drugs, substitute speed for food, and do their fair share to contribute to the current VD epidemic. Sometimes they die as victims of violence or bad drugs or drunken driving. Run-tos face risks.

But until run-tos experience the negative consequences of their life-style, it's their parents who suffer. Parents are tormented by their fears for their child's well-being and usually at their wits' end when they hear from them. One parent writes:

> I awaken in the middle of the night, shivering and shaken. Sometimes I can't remember what I was just dreaming, but often I can. Sally's always in the dream and she's been hurt or is about to be.
>
> Other times I'm afraid of the telephone. When it rings, I'm reluctant to pick it up. I expect the hospital or the police, telling me she's been hurt or is in trouble. It's happened several times, so I expect it to happen again.
>
> By the time she finally calls, I'm so happy that she's alright that I take her home without any questions asked. I know it's stupid, but that's what happens.

Not the kind of letter one would expect from a drunken, abusing parent who doesn't want his or her kid, yet it is typical of the tens of thousands of letters and phone calls we have received from parents. Still, the pop psychological misconceptions prevail: if a kid runs away, the parents must be doing something wrong. Even their closest relatives may doubt them.

"We are parents of a son who runs away when we say or do anything he doesn't like.

"He usually stays at a friend's house or his grandma's or dear aunt's. We are always placed in the position of being villains. They all think he's wonderful; they should live with him for more than a week. What would they do when he didn't get up for school, or threw a string of profanity at you, or smoked pot in your living room?

"I asked him to pick up his sweater from the middle of the floor, he says OK and walks out and has been gone for two days. Then we start to phone around and finally find him, he gets on the phone and dictates the terms he's going to come home to. We usually give in, but to tell you the truth, at this point we're thinking of asking some of those dear sweet people who think he's so wonderful to keep him. Please send information."

Few of us expect to have children who run away. Most of us think of ourselves as responsible, caring adults, not ogres who drive our kids into the streets. But when it happens, even the strongest parents are shaken. We lose confidence in ourselves and search our souls for the "reasons" for our child's actions. We feel frightened and ashamed and guilty, but most of all we feel helpless. We will do almost anything to get our children back. We are willing to forgive them and indulge them to somehow keep them home and keep them safe.

A mother in a televised town meeting in Minnesota stood up and tearfully pleaded with her thirteen-year-old daughter to come home. She cried, "We love you. We can work anything out if you'll come home. We miss you." She broke down as she held up a picture of her sweet-looking youngster. The whole audience cried and people embraced her. After the show three telephone calls came in, each reporting the girl in the same area. The mother and father and a reporter rushed out to follow up on the calls.

Another mother at our TOUGHLOVE Weekend Workshop in Seattle told us how her daughter always returned from her three-week run-tos practically naked. Mom would feel bad, but was relieved that her daughter had returned and would rush out to buy her warm shirts, jeans, a coat, shoes, and a new hairbrush. After a short respite, her daughter left again with her new things, only to return nearly naked three weeks later.

As parents of run-tos, we become so anxious to please our kids, to show them that we love them, and to receive their love in return. We succumb and cater to our kids so they will want to stay home and grow up in ways we think will help them. We think that if we give enough or act loving enough or hurt enough or angry enough, the kids will stay. Despite all our efforts, the kids don't see or hear us. Their eyes and minds are elsewhere, thinking about good times on the street, partying, excitement.

"Our problem is a daughter who is a habitual runaway," wrote one father. "She is probably using drugs and may be prostituting to support herself. She drifts home when she is tired or ill (thus the third test for VD in six months) or is hungry. Then she disappears again. Her eighteenth birthday was several months ago.

"She has been counseled by her church, her school, a counseling service, and her doctors. None of this had any effect.

"We are desperate. The strain of worry about her is unbearable at times. Can your program be of help to us?"

Sixteen-year-old Donna said, "When you stay out, you don't care about your family. When you go home, everyone's mad at you or walking on egg-shells. It's like a bummer and you feel like leaving again. I got it in my head that everything my parents did and said was wrong and crazy and I was right and could do anything I wanted. I would just go home to rest."

Kids use their running away as a threat, as a manipulative tool. At a recent gathering in New England, we spoke to a large group about TOUGH-LOVE. One woman asked if TOUGHLOVE could help with her daughter.

"I'm so upset. I feel TOUGHLOVE is my last resort. My daughter threatened to kill herself. She was hospitalized and we all saw a psychiatrist who we are still meeting with. She no longer talks about suicide, but for the first three months of this year we were held captive by her threats. Now whenever things don't go well, she threatens to run away. The psychiatrist says to let her have her own way. Our whole family is scared and resentful. Sometimes I think I'll kill myself if this doesn't end."

People in the audience reached out to her, telling her they had the same problem, inviting her to their TOUGHLOVE group. After the meeting we overheard people talking to her.

"I told her if she chose to leave she would have to work her way back."

"I finally said he was free to leave but he could not live an isolated existence in our home."

"I informed the juvenile officer that he was planning to leave."

"Please come to our group. It's the support that helps."

When a child in his or her teens runs away from home, we panic. We envisage the worst. Sordid street scenes fill our minds. Threats to run away terrorize us. We feel blackmailed. So when our child comes home, we surrender our confidence and dignity to prevent the reality of our fears.

Kids run away for a variety of reasons. Some are abused. Most are into drugs and partying, won't manage their lives at home, school, or work, won't face problems they have created for themselves, won't stand the pain and anxiety of growing up, make impulsive decisions, or simply want their own way. So they leave. After all, splitting, separating, divorcing, and looking for new relationships are acceptable cultural norms for adults as well as young people. Leaving has become a popular way to solve problems.

Marilou, who has lived in several group homes and foster homes said, "Running becomes a habit. You know you never need to be cornered. You can always get out. Just walking away makes you feel better. You never have to see anything you don't want to. It gets so the only time you feel comfortable is when you're running."

John told his mother, "Everything at home was a hassle. I was only interested in partying. I couldn't handle school, work, or anything else. Just being out was easier."

In TOUGHLOVE our first task is to confront the habit of running away. We put aside our shame and fear and go public. We call the police and the school and discuss the whole situation with other parents in our TOUGHLOVE group. Some kids are stunned when they find that their parents have involved others in the community and they stop running away. Unfortunately, many don't stop that easily. Nonetheless, it's the first step toward finding a solution. Notifying the authorities is the appropriate legal procedure and helps parents avoid complications, like receiving fines for their child's truancy during the time they are on the run.

Many parents are disappointed by the reaction of the police. Although they will probably list the child's name with the federal runaway register (which acts as a central clearinghouse for identifying runaway kids), the police are so overwhelmed by the number of runaways that they simply don't have the time or energy to do much more.

On the other hand, where TOUGHLOVE groups have established cooperative relationships with police departments and where police see that their assistance is part of an overall plan to change the child's behavior, they become much more involved. They too are frustrated by the helplessness that they as adults feel in dealing with these young people and they're delighted when they see some meaningful results.

Besides informing the police each time a child leaves, parents can brainstorm other steps with their TOUGHLOVE group. Parents who frantically drive all over searching for their kid, who always comes home in a day or two, may work out a plan for responding to their kid's return. With the support of other parents, they decide to grit their teeth and wait. Parents who always wait helplessly for their kid to come home may go out and find the kid. Changing responses stymies manipulative kids who know how to push their parents' buttons to get what they want.

Like our friend in Seattle who bought her daughter a new wardrobe when she returned. She told us that she finally realized that supplying new clothes for her daughter was providing a "runaway kit" which allowed her daughter to live comfortably on the street. Mom changed her response. No more runaway kits.

Other parents decide on a much tougher change. They refuse to take their child back home when he or she returns. Taking this step without a TOUGH-LOVE group or plan is not using a TOUGHLOVE solution. TOUGHLOVE is loving as well as tough. The support and involvement of other adults with the run-to and the family is most helpful in stopping destructive and hurtful patterns. A mother in Illinois wrote us about her new reaction to her sixteen-year-old son who had run away so many times that she accepted his comings and goings.

"When I came to TOUGHLOVE, I realized that I had grown accustomed to his behavior, but I really didn't have to accept it and that I wasn't really comfortable with it but I was just helpless about it.

"When my son came home from one of his treks, I met him at the door with his belongings and told him I had arranged for him to stay at someone else's house. We got in the car and I drove him to my support's house. He stayed the night, he seemed bewildered.

"He was informed that I was not willing to take him home if he continued to leave. He was told that he needed to get his drug habit taken care of and given the name of a D&A [drug and alcohol] unit he could call. He did it. I know we have a long way to go, but we've begun."

The mother of Laurel, the seventeen-year-old who told us that life on the streets was too hard, wrote to us at the time of Laurel's return about how she was directing her daughter instead of accepting her.

"My group has helped me set up guidelines for her. First of all, she has to go to our local runaway house and report in; they have agreed to work with us. Second, my TOUGHLOVE surrogate parents would come to the first meeting at the shelter. They would explain that she had to have a D&A evaluation.

"That she needed to be drug-free, even if it meant going to a drug program, and that doing these things would prove she was in good faith and not just manipulating—then we'd get together.

"I've got my fingers crossed, but right now my heart is beating a mile a minute because my TOUGH-LOVE support person told me Laurel has signed herself into the shelter."

None of these responses are pat solutions. Each child and each situation requires thoughtfulness. Refusing to take home a sixteen- or seventeen-year-old who clearly has survival skills is not without its risks, but leaving a younger adolescent who is just beginning a runaway pattern on the streets might be like leading a lamb to slaughter.

Margo, a widow, came to a TOUGHLOVE group the week after her thirteen-year-old, Barbara, ran away. Margo told the group that she had found out that her youngster had been spending time with an older man. Margo went to the police with a description of the man. She also went to "the strip" (an area characterized by porno shops and prostitutes) and showed her daughter's picture around. She confirmed that her daughter was hanging around the strip and staying with a thirty-three-year-old man, whose address she obtained. She went back to the police, who reported that no one was home when they checked, but promised Margo that they would return.

As she told her story to the other TOUGHLOVE parents, one man asked if she wanted help in getting her daughter right now. Of course she was thrilled. Four fathers and Margo left the meeting and went to the apartment where Barbara was staying. No one responded to their knock, so they went outside and waited in the car.

Eventually, Margo spotted Barbara standing with a group of kids. The men approached Barbara, escorted her to her mother's waiting car, jumped in, and Margo drove off. They were gone in a matter of minutes. Margo pressed charges against the older man and Barbara is now home, being thirteen again.

Other parents involve the legal system by having their run-tos declared wards of the court. Young people who are placed in this legal situation are labeled by a variety of names: PINS ("people in need of supervision"), CHINS ("children in need of supervision"), incorrigibles, ungovernables, and status offenders. No one likes taking this step.

"My daughter is only twelve. She was staying out all night and being violent at home. I had to take out a petition on her. I couldn't see any other choice."

Taking this step forces kids to recognize that parents won't tolerate their behavior. It also formally involves government social service agencies, which can help parents by mandating treatment and counseling for their child. Finally, it provides leverage with some kids who are willing to make necessary changes so that they can move back home with their families.

Involving the legal system is not a panacea and it may not be easy. Social service agencies, overburdened by the cost of so many troubled adolescents in placement, are frequently reluctant to take on more kids and may fight the parents in court. Teenagers who are not yet hardened may move deeper into antisocial life-styles, influenced by other kids they meet in programs and institutions. But for kids who are behaving as intolerably as ours, we need to use the available resources and petitioning the court may be very appropriate.

Once again, where TOUGHLOVE groups have forged healthy relationships with agencies in the community, parents will find the courts and caseworkers more cooperative. Youth agencies may be more comfortable accepting a new placement when the overall strategy is to help the young person change and return home. They come to realize that the TOUGHLOVE parents are not trying to dump their kid on someone else, but are searching for solutions. A judge in Pennsylvania, for instance, refers parents to TOUGHLOVE because he knows "TOUGHLOVE parents are folks who care."

Sometimes a telephone call comes into our TOUGHLOVE office from parents who are trying to find a TOUGHLOVE group in a location distant from where they themselves live. Their run-to son or daughter has been detained or arrested and they want to arrange for some long-distance coordination with other concerned parents. We have excerpted a letter from a seventeen-year-old who wrote to us months after his parents made just such a phone call.

One day I got caught shoplifting in Michigan and got taken to the police station. I called home and my folks said they couldn't help me. So I stayed right in their jail. Then this man and woman come in and tell me they came to see me because they belong to TOUGHLOVE and it was up to me if I was going to go to detention or clean up my act. It was weird. They told me they knew I was in trouble because my mother and stepfather are members of TOUGHLOVE and called them. They give me the night to think over whether I'll plead guilty and go to treatment or detention. I choose detention and I'm miserable and these people and another woman come to see me. I've got to get out. The hearing comes up. These strange people come to court and they know everything I've done. I can't believe it. They say if I'm willing to go to treatment and not run away, my parents will take me back. So I went to a twenty-eight-day rehab program. My parents flew in to see me and have a meeting. They let me know that I had to register in school before I came home or live with another TOUGHLOVE family until I found a job. I went to a foster home after rehab. I got my G.E.D. [a high school equivalency diploma obtained by passing an examination] and a job at Gino's. I'm going home next week. I'm still stubborn, but I'm not partying anymore or running. It's too much of a hassle. TOUGHLOVE has been good for my parents—it makes them strong.

For most parents the initial thought of confronting our run-to son or daughter seems frightening. If we fear a young person is starting to live a desperate life of drug addiction or prostitution or theft, then we want to keep our child home where we think he or she is safe. We avoid rocking the boat by making even minor demands because we might break the last tenuous thread and we will lose our child forever. So we maintain our child's cruel life and our fears rather than take the risk of losing him or her.

But that is exactly the risk we have to take. A risk that we take by saying, "Our home and our family are worth coming home to, not because you're burned out and need a place to rest, but because we love and value you. If you want to be a real member of our family, this is what you have to do." Then we present the plan we have worked out with our TOUGHLOVE group, a plan that fits us, our community, and our support group.

We take a risk by asking our runaway or run-to to choose between family life and the sloppy life he or she is leading. And we get to the point that we accept the choice, even if it means the loss of our child for now. The accommodations we have made have already put us on the brink of losing our child. We will need the support of other parents who struggled with the same hard demands for their own kids and who are there for us, parents who will hold our hand and ease the pain and anxiety that we feel at

times like these. The kind of parents who make
TOUGHLOVE solutions possible.

Some run-tos can be tough, resourceful, and
streetwise. They may be far down the path and hard
to stop. Sometimes it takes years until they get too
tired to hustle. Even then, most parents will go the
extra mile if their kid makes the first move back
toward a healthy life. Unfortunately, there are some
kids who will never change.

The prognosis is better for a beginning run-to.
If he's the kind of kid who turns to grandma, auntie,
family friends, or the ex-spouse for shelter, parents
need to get all his support people to agree to refuse
him shelter until he has straightened things out at
home. Sometimes they are reluctant, probably because they have doubts about who is really at fault.
The best way to handle such friends or relatives is to
ask them to come to a TOUGHLOVE group. If they
refuse, let them take him in for a while, long enough
to wear out his goody-goody act. When they experience the same rotten behavior that parents have
suffered, they will readily agree to help him solve his
problems at home.

> I always thought my daughter and son-in-
> law were not understanding enough of my grand-
> son, Henry. They suggested he come and live
> with me for a while and I was delighted. He was
> perfect for three days. Then I started to see
> what his parents complained about. I tried talk-
> ing with him, but when some of my jewelry
> disappeared I sent him home and joined my
> daughter and her husband in TOUGHLOVE.

And if he does manage to live there effectively,
perhaps the problem is manageable and his parents

might reassess the situation, working out a way for him to stay there longer.

> My son Caleb moved in with his aunt. She lives in the next town and Caleb always liked to visit her. I kept waiting for him to cause enough trouble to get kicked out, but he's doing OK. It's been three months now and I feel like a real failure, but I can live with that better than I could live with a drunk and stoned son.

The latter situation, however, is extremely rare. Most kids blow out in a couple of weeks.

People who harbor a run-to but are not friends or family should be contacted as well. Parents or their TOUGHLOVE group members may find that they can change people's perception by explaining the problem and asking for help. If people do not respond favorably, parents may try several extremely effective techniques: ask the do-gooders if they are prepared to assume permanent legal custody for the run-to or—if the situation warrants—threaten to press charges for "corrupting the morals of a minor" or ask the police to investigate. It's amazing how quickly most people will send the kid packing when they are faced with legal complications.

The more parents can undermine a run-to's resources, the more hassle parents can create for the run-to's allies, the more fearful the run-to is that the police are involved, the more embarrassed he is about everyone hearing about his behavior, the more likely that he will come around. Ironically, parental shame is the runaway's biggest asset because it keeps parents from contacting other people. Once parents free themselves and go public, they find that they have a great many options and supports they didn't realize they had.

Members of one TOUGHLOVE group contacted us about a successful innovation they used. They printed "UNWANTED" posters. The posters each bore a photograph of a run-to with the word "UN-WANTED" in large bold letters. Underneath the photo was the name of the run-to, the telephone number of a group contact person, and an inscription which read, "This child is UNWANTED in your home. He does not have permission to stay away from home, so please do not become an accessory to a RUNAWAY by taking him in. If you want to help him, call this telephone number to report his location." They put the posters up in banks, supermarkets, post offices, and other highly trafficked locations. The kids were incensed, but it dramatically cut down on the number of kids who stayed away from home without permission. Although the group printed posters for only three different run-tos, the word got around to others. It even stopped one fellow who stayed out only on Saturday nights.

When a run-to wants to return home, parents have the opportunity to make demands. Sometimes parents develop elaborate contracts with ten, twenty, even fifty or a hundred items that their child must agree to. The items include simple courtesies and routine chores that their acting-out child has avoided for months or years, so parents then try to write them all down. Such lists are too unwieldy for all concerned. Besides, most kids know what normal family life demands and listing so many requirements on paper implies that maybe they don't. The situation is a setup for "I don't remember. Tell me again."

Parents need to start simply. At the outset they should cite, in writing, three or four conditions for returning home and a specific plan for meeting again, for reviewing the situation, and for setting further demands. A teenager might be asked to sign a contract that reads as follows:

1. I will stay at Mr. and Mrs. X's home and discuss these demands with their family.
2. I will make and keep an appointment for a drug and alcohol evaluation and abide by the recommendations.
3. I will not run away this week.
4. I will meet and plan next week's contract at such and such a time and place with my parents and two other TOUGHLOVE parents.

Each week parents can focus on new issues and add them to the contract and old items can be dropped as they have been met so that goals are kept clear and simple.

Some people have asked us whether a contract should include demands on parents. We don't think so. The parents are providing room, board, and loving concern. That's an awful lot to give a son or daughter who has been rude, cruel, violent, dishonest, and rotten to his family. Somewhere down the line, when the kid has dealt with his or her behavior, held a job, or attended school successfully and has consistently demonstrated good faith, then parents can agree to some demands. The exception is when the TOUGHLOVE support people feel that the parents are unreasonable and need to back off on some issues, like an early curfew or excessive chores. That's why other folks are involved in setting up and reviewing the contract: to offer some balance and perspective in a highly emotional situation.

A returning runaway or run-to has a real commitment to make and will need someplace to live until the meeting is held. Not permitting a child to return home before he or she makes the commitment to change helps the family avoid another round of manipulation and wishful thinking. A local runaway shelter—if available—is a wonderful resource for such situations. But runaway shelters are not available in many communities or are closing due to funding cutbacks. That's where the TOUGHLOVE group proves so useful: parents provide shelter for each other's children in emergency situations. Ironically, even acting-out kids are usually on their best behavior in other people's homes, at least for a week or two.

Refusing to take a child home has legal implications. Usually parents avoid hassles by arranging for alternative housing, at a runaway shelter or a friend's home. But sometimes they run into problems.

When the police called, Joey had been gone for ten days. Jane and I were asleep. They said they had Joey at the station and that he had been wandering around downtown. They thought he was stoned on something. Anyway, they wanted us to come right down to the station and pick him up. They were shocked when I said that we would prefer if they would keep him there for the night.

Then some other policeman got on the phone and screamed at me that it was illegal to abandon our kid and that we had better get down there right away or he'd be over to arrest us for neglecting our child. I tried to explain, but he hung up on me.

We didn't know what to do. We didn't want to bother anybody in our TOUGHLOVE group in the middle of the night. We had hoped to get someone to help us the next morning. But we didn't want to get arrested. I could just picture Joey listening to the cop screaming at us. It made me angry. So I decided to call Bob Clinch.

Bob explained that this had happened before. The TOUGHLOVE group had even sent its Action Team to explain our philosophy to the police, but the Chief just lectured them on their responsibilities as parents. He said that the Chief interpreted the law to mean that a child had the right to return to his own home, no matter what, and that the child could not go to someone else's home instead. Anyway, Bob said he'd be right over to pick me up. He said he knew how to handle it.

When we got to the station, I went in alone. Joey was cocky as a rooster. He grinned at me when I walked in, thinking he'd won again. He looked more exhausted than stoned, like he could fall asleep standing. I signed the release papers and left. I told Joey I was here with a friend and we got in the car. We didn't say a word to Joey and he fell asleep in the back of the car. We drove to my house, just as Bob and I had agreed. Joey didn't even wake up, so it made the plan easy. I just got out and Bob drove off with Joey.

Bob told me what happened the next day. He said I should have seen Joey's face when he woke him and told him he was staying at his house. I wish I had been there. Anyway, the Clinches kept him there for two days until he agreed to go to the school counselor and work out a plan to attend school and make up his work. He knew we weren't kidding about not taking him home.

This story had a happy ending, but that's not always the case. Some young people refuse alternative housing and take to the streets again. Usually for a short while, sometimes for a long while. And occasionally forever. That, of course, is a parent's greatest fear. But a young person who values his raunchy life-style over his family is a young person who is not fit to live with. His parents are not responsible for his decision to leave and they need not burden themselves with guilt. People do not have to live with monsters, even if those monsters are their children. Taking an abusive kid back without a commitment to personal change is not even helpful to the kid—and certainly not helpful to the rest of the family.

Fortunately, most kids do come around. The younger the better, for it seems that older kids are more resourceful at staying away and are less frightened about leaving their homes. Nonetheless, the strategy has worked with young people in their twenties who are still mooching off their parents and using their home as a crash pad. Dependent on their parents, they are emotional adolescents in adult bodies.

Run-tos are so prevalent in our society in part because people are willing to take them in. Many people believe these young con artists and let them stay in their homes without ever checking with their parents. They believe they are helping, when in fact they are not. TOUGHLOVE groups can help to change this pattern by educating the public, as one TOUGHLOVE group did by distributing the following guidelines:

1. Don't allow kids to stay in your home until you've checked their story with their parents.

2. If you hear from your child that a friend is hiding or has run away, call his parents to report his whereabouts. You are not betraying your child's confidence. You are just letting him know that some things are too hurtful to be secrets.

3. If a kid wants to stay with you and you are willing to take him in, get together with his parents.

You may be helpful, since some kids do better in other people's homes.

4. If a teenager seems to be unconnected and wandering, call his or her parents or the police or the local runaway shelter.

5. If a teenager claims to be abused, call the appropriate social service agency and ask them to check it out.

6. Try talking to a kid who seems to be on the run. Offer to go home with him.

Running away has become a common phenomenon in our society. The number of kids who are on the run has overwhelmed the police and social service agencies who deal with them. TOUGHLOVE techniques, although they may seem harsh to people who are unfamiliar with the situation, produce positive results and have reunited many a family with their wayward child. The following excerpted letter is from just such a child.

One night I fell asleep at a friend's house and didn't get home till the next day when I snuck into my house early in the morning. I thought I'd get killed, but that didn't happen. I just got the cold shoulder from my parents. So that was when I decided I could do what I wanted and what I wanted to do was to stay out and party. I'm seventeen and I've got a lot of friends.

I stayed out more and more and when I went home I get hassled so bad I started to break up the house. So my parents they leave me alone.

In my area I still seem like a nice kid to my friends' parents, so I can spend a weekend or a couple of days hanging out at friends' houses. I also act like I'm going to school and I leave the houses I stay in and when the parents go to work I climb in a window my friends leave open for me.

I also hang around some guys who have their own place. I go home to shower or get clothes. That's one thing about sleeping around or living on the street. You lose a lot of clothes.

Well, this goes on for a few months. One day I go home to get cleaned up and the doors are locked. My father comes to the door and tells me I'm not welcome in his house until I clean up my act. He hands me a note with names with telephone numbers on it of people to call if I want help. I am furious. Who the hell does he think he is? I'll show him.

I go to a friend's house and crash. The next day when they go to work, I break the basement window, shower, eat, kick in my bedroom door, take my brother's guitar, smash a lamp, and break some dishes. I feel good now.

By the way, I go to school almost every day. The next day at school the assistant principal calls me in and tells me I'm not doing shit in school, I'm failing, and they know I'm not living at home. I have one week to get my act together or leave. I'm pissed as hell. What's this, a conspiracy!

Anyway, I go home to a girlfriend's house and her mother tells me I'm not welcome in her house, she heard I ripped off my parents' house and that she doesn't want me around.

Out on the street I figure I'll stay downtown at the Mall for a while. I'm feeling paranoid. Every time a cop passed, I jumped and hid.

Finally, at ten o'clock I'm so drunk I don't know where to go. A dude I know says I can sleep in his car until he goes to work in the morning. I am still smashed in the morning, but I go to school anyway. I want to see my girlfriend. In school the assistant principal says I'm drunk and orders me to sit on a bench outside his office. He tells me to get my behind to a D&A clinic and gives me the number to call.

I leave now I've got two cards and again sleep in my friend's car. In the morning I go to school and it starts all over again and so it goes for two more days. By this time I'm sick, dirty, all of my friends are being hassled, and I'm about to be kicked out of school. I look at the cards in my pocket and call these other people who agree to meet with me.

Well, you know they were TOUGHLOVE parents and they helped me to get my head cleaned up. I spend four weeks in a D&A rehab and then went home. I graduated high school and it's been uphill ever since. I don't know why I thought my parents hated me, except maybe they should have.

I go to AA a few times a week and in the fall I start community college and I bought my brother a new guitar.

Runaways and run-tos have become a major problem in communities all over North America. Porno strips, male and female prostitution, drugs and violence are all outcomes of this pervasive leaving home phenomenon. TOUGHLOVE asks all of us to shoulder the responsibility and develop answers to stop the destruction of young people's lives and the communities they live in. Running away is not an acceptable solution to family problems. TOUGHLOVE is one answer that has helped.

CHAPTER 6:

Sex

"Do you think it's all right for a teenager to just visit a gynecologist when she feels well, isn't pregnant, and isn't asking for birth control?" asked Marie, a woman in her fifties. She was talking to Francine, a woman in her early forties, and Ruth, in her mid-thirties. "Ellen, my eighteen-year-old, told me she was going to see the gynecologist to make sure she was OK internally. I don't know. I only went to the gynecologist when I was married and pregnant, not when I was a girl."

Both Ruth and Francine agreed that an internal exam is part of routine health maintenance. Francine said, "My kids went when they were in their late teens—or at least one of them went, but that was about birth control. I think it's right that young girls should go, but ..." Francine seemed unsure.

Ruth spoke up. "I plan to take Wendy when she starts menstruating. I want her to get used to going to the gynecologist for other than birth control. I want her to see it as part of caring for her body."

"I come from the generation that only acknowledged sex after we got married," Marie said laughingly. "Vaginas and their whereabouts were a secret. Getting your period was an embarrassment. And 'doing it' was only for bad girls. If you got pregnant, getting an abortion was almost impossible. In fact, it was almost unthinkable. A shotgun wedding was the usual solution."

"By the time my children were teenagers," said Francine, "the pill was available, abortion was legal, and adolescent sexuality was discussed openly. Nobody talked in terms of sexual promiscuity, only sexual activity. As a parent I was aware of all this recognition of kids' sexuality, but I didn't know how to help my daughters handle it. I looked at the way I managed my sexuality and sex role and didn't want them to suffer the ill effect I thought repression had on me. But I didn't know how to handle the new information in the culture and meanwhile my kids got into problems. When I listen to you, Ruth, I feel jealous that you seem to have the blueprint that I lacked. You seem to be able to help your daughter deal with her body changes, her growing sexuality, without her feeling like some kind of machine that needs birth control."

Sex, sex role, and sexuality. The last few decades have witnessed dramatic shifts in values and attitudes, from the austerity of the Victorian to the raw candor of the Aquarian. Adults accept the disparity between then and now and search for new ways to be, ways that will help their children navigate past today's perils while avoiding the hazards of yesterday.

Dear David and Phyllis:

I just finished reading your book, *TOUGH-LOVE*, and you made me really do some serious thinking about the way I was raised and the way my own children are growing up in the eighties. I was married in 1960 after leading a fairly normal, sheltered life. We didn't really know much about drugs or sex or the problems of managing a family. I guess our parents protected us from a lot, but I also know that so many things weren't common knowledge like they are today.

During the sixties there were so many changes that affected my own life. Our friends started smoking pot and there was suddenly so much information about sex. I think that our lives changed because of all the information that became available. I know that I began to feel a lot of pressure to try drugs and new sexual activities because it became a matter of "Everybody's doing it." Things that had been alluded to in literature and gossip and dirty jokes suddenly became the "norm" for people that I'd always known and respected.

A lot of the new things I felt pressured to try I found that I really liked. We began to use pot socially and I don't think we ever abused the drug by letting it interfere with our daily lives. We also tried a lot of new sexual things and I liked that too. There were some things that we tried and rejected and some things that we didn't do. But we didn't care that some of our friends were doing things that were not what we wanted to do—like switchies and orgies and drugs like cocaine and ludes. I guess it became our ethic to accept other people's life-styles if it didn't interfere with our own.

So now I wonder about my own kids and the pressure that they feel from the culture and the media. Do they think that it is normal for young kids to be having sex and that everyone has to try drugs? I've really been thinking about how different my life would be if I had not been exposed to so much information about things my own parents never heard of. Is this what is happening to my own kids? How do I protect them?

I felt like I received all this information when I was an adult and could make some decisions about what I chose to do and chose not to do. I had a lot of self-confidence and a strong feeling about "who I am" when I received new information. But these kids are not experienced enough to start making choices that are offered to them today. When I said, "Everybody's doing it" to my mother, she could laugh at me and say, "I really doubt that." But my kids don't even have to say, "Everybody's doing it" to me. I already know that!

It scares me to think that they will make choices without having adequate decision-making skills and certain life-styles will become adopted as their own by habit, not by choice. I know how much pressure I used to feel—and I was in my late twenties. They are in their teens and I think the pressure to try drugs and sex is immensely stronger than it was twenty years ago. It scares me.

This letter expresses the concerns of an eighties mother and contrasts with the concerns of an earlier generation. For instance, in the fifties worried parents wrote to advice columnists expressing concern about their child's behavior. Letters began with "My sixteen-year-old daughter is going steady . . ." and ended with "I fear she will be trapped into early marriage and responsibility." Lifelong monogamy was the norm and "going steady" was practice for the real thing. Kids could rationalize "doing it" if they were going steady and in love. Parents' greatest fears were about shotgun weddings and births before nine months of married life.

Girls were assumed to be taken advantage of, unless they were promiscuous, nymphomaniacs, or just "easy," while boys were assumed to be struggling with an all-engulfing sex drive that needed to be curbed. Prophylactics were the only form of birth control available and were still illegal in some states. Young men felt the trauma of privately asking the druggist for "protection." Repression was the order of the day.

Around 1960 we looked up from our missionary position and saw sex from a new vantage point. The pill, a form of birth control which gave women reliable discretion over pregnancy, supposedly made sex fun for everyone. Action and experimentation became the new order of the day. *The Joy of Sex* replaced *The Kinsey Report*. Sexual norms and values shifted as magazines and movies moved from revealing breast and buttock to exposing vagina and penis.

Adults struggled with issues of sexuality. The institution of marriage itself was scrutinized and challenged as monogamy (with illicit male affairs) gave way to open marriages, communal marriages, swinging, and mate-swapping. Experiencing oneself to the fullest prevailed over repression, but indulgence was accompanied by its own struggles and agonies. "If it feels good, do it" sounded attractive as a slogan but it was not without its negative consequences. The number of marriages each year was soon equaled by the number of divorces. The number of kids living with both natural parents was equaled by the number of kids who weren't.

"Teen Sex, Too Much Too Soon?" was an article recently featured on the cover of *Ms.* magazine. Not only adults have experienced greater sexual freedom. A lack of age-appropriate sexual behavior means more thirteen-year-old pregnancies, more fourteen-year-old kids contemplating abortion, more fifteen-year-old mothers on the welfare rolls. Children making difficult decisions and facing major responsibilities for which they are unprepared.

> We are now grandparents. Our fourteen-year-old daughter has had a baby. We will raise him and love him. We are in great pain and shame, but we cannot in good conscience do otherwise.
> What bothers us now is that our fourteen-year-old child has had this womanly experience. We would like to talk this over with other parents and be able to talk to our daughter in a meaningful way. After all, she is still a child. We know God has a reason. . . .

A generation of young people has grown up amid the chaos of our society's changing values. Parents are now trying to raise children in uncharted waters without maps or navigational instruments. The sexual revolution has shattered the old limits and has not yet defined new ones. When traditions give way suddenly, the void is quickly filled by the cheap and the sensational. Pornography, sexual exploitation of the young, sexual violence, prostitution, and venereal disease are commonplace.

We don't mean to suggest that the sexual revolution has been only negative. But it's had its casualties and TOUGHLOVE parents and their kids are among them. They are usually the parents of daughters, since the liberation has not freed women from bearing the major consequences of sex.

Most of us make pronouncements based on human rights or religious values on subjects such as birth control, abortion, single parenthood, homosexuality, and teenage pregnancy. But when your own child is pregnant or homosexual or promiscuous, the abstractions and intellectualizations fade away.

I do not believe in unsigned letters, but I think that you will understand why I choose to remain anonymous after you read my story. After seeing you on television this morning, I feel that I must share this story with you, for I know that you will understand what can happen to a mother when her daughter is in trouble.

I am the mother of seven children, ages thirteen to twenty-eight. All but two of the children are out of the house now, but raising them was no easy task, as well you must know. We had good times and bad times, but mostly my husband and I rejoiced in the blessings of our children. We were very strict with the children as they grew up and the effort was worthwhile because they all graduated from Catholic school and either got married, went right to work or to college. We are now the proud grandparents of four beautiful babies.

My youngest child is only thirteen, a little girl who has been pampered and spoiled by the whole family. I always thought that she was the most overprotected one of them all and was definitely everyone's favorite. Imagine my shock when I discovered—quite by accident—that she was pregnant. I reacted just as you said parents do—I knew it must be a mistake. She had been acting sickly for a few weeks, but refused to see a doctor, saying it was just a flu going around school. Looking back, I think I thought about pregnancy, but knew it was impossible for my baby, so dismissed the thought immediately. When I found a pregnancy test kit box in her trash can, I felt panic.

I remember the words repeating in my head for hours—"This can't be, this can't be, this can't be." Somehow, saying it over and over kept other, more terrible thoughts from entering my head. I felt sick and wanted to vomit. My head pounded. My heart felt as though it would choke me and burst. I knew that I had to do something, but didn't know what it should be.

How could I tell for sure? Maybe it was for a friend or her sister—or she had found it some-place and brought it home to look at in the privacy of her room. I convinced myself that it couldn't be true, but started to worry about how to ask her about the box without offending and alienating her. I became so sure that there was some strange coincidence that I decided not to do anything.

But I noticed that she slept when she got home from school. Her appetite varied from refusing to eat to "pigging out." I told myself that this was normal for a teenager. But I could not remember when she had last had a period and her body was changing. I began to feel sick everyday. I had headaches and couldn't sleep at night. I lost twelve pounds in two weeks.

One morning I heard my little girl vomiting in the bathroom and I walked right in. I said, "Are you pregnant?" and she started to cry and couldn't stop. I sat on the edge of the bathtub with her in my lap, holding her so tightly I

thought she'd break. I prayed for God to give
me an answer, to make this not be true for my
baby. My religion has always been the center of
my life and I had always been faithful to God. I
asked my daughter to pray with me, to ask God's
help. In my heart, I prayed for Him to make
her have a miscarriage, right there in the bathroom.

I do not believe in abortion for anyone and
had even been active in a local organization to
combat liberal abortion laws. The only solution
in my heart and mind at that time was to ask
God to end this pregnancy. I knew that I had to
help my little girl, so I told her to get in bed and
we would talk as soon as my husband and son
left the house. When I went back to her room, I
snuggled into her bed with her and asked her
how she knew that she was pregnant. She told
me about having sex with a boy at parties for the
last five months and about missing two periods.
I felt no anger because I was talking to a baby
who did not even yet have the body of a woman.

As I held her in the bed, I felt her softness
and smelled the little girl sweetness of her. I
knew that she could not have a baby. I could
not let her whole life be ruined for mistakes she
did not yet understand. I could not talk to my
husband or even my older daughter about this.
I went to the telephone book and looked up the
number of a clinic in our state capital and called
them to ask for advice. We drove there for the
testing and I made arrangments to have the
abortion, God forgive me. I told my daughter
that we had to keep this our secret because no
one else would understand. I told her that it was
my decision, not hers, and she was not responsible for the pregnancy or the abortion. I cannot

believe that a loving God would want a little
girl's life to be ruined forever by mistakes she
did not understand. Forty-five years of faith and
conviction were shaken for me when the girl in
trouble was my own daughter. I know in my
head that I have committed a sin, but my heart
tells me that there was no choice. I pray that
God will forgive me.

At a TOUGHLOVE Workshop a mother told us
of her struggle. Her nineteen-year-old son was totally ignoring a seventeen-year-old girl that he made
pregnant. The girl kept coming over to the house
and the woman would try to get her son to talk to
her, but instead he would leave. His mother felt she
had to talk to and take care of this young woman.
The other parents urged the mother to recognize
that she was not responsible for the pregnancy and
that instead she should demand that her son take
responsibility. Even if he refused, they felt it was
important for her to let her son know where she
stood on the issue. The woman agreed, went home,
and confronted her son. He took the young woman
for an abortion, a solution that the reader may or
may not like. Nonetheless, the solution was a choice
based on the young couple's own behavior, not someone else's, and abortion is the solution they chose.

Most of us hope that young people only need to
get in trouble once to learn life's lessons. Unfortunately, many people make the same mistakes more
than once.

Please send information to my sister. She
needs help. I took her for an abortion last year
and she thinks she is pregnant again now. She's
really a wonderful person, but thinks that every
guy who shows her some attention is in love with

her and she falls in love with him. I can understand one mistake, but not another and I can't stand the thought of driving her to another abortion. If you have any pamphlets that will make her understand how to stay cool, please send them. Thank you for caring about kids.

Although abortion is not supposed to be a method of birth control, this young woman and her sister are facing a crisis now and will not be open to a lecture on morality. If it's true that contraceptives have to fit a person's life-style, then for the teens whose lives are unsettled, they don't fit at all. Their denial of their own sexuality and sexual behaviors leads to a lot of grief.

Many young people who feel lost in adolescence turn to sex for security, to prove to themselves that they are wanted and valuable or that they are grown up. They also indulge themselves simply because sex feels good. For whatever reasons, their sexual activity challenges parents who are struggling to reassess and define guidelines.

One TOUGHLOVE group addressed the issue of teenage sexuality by inviting a series of guest speakers for the information portion of their weekly meetings. Planned Parenthood, local mental health clinics, and other agencies provided knowledgeable people. The group then defined a set of guidelines together to help parents decide where they stand:

1. Kids sixteen and under are too young for sexual intercourse.

2. Kids over sixteen should be told what their responsibilities are toward themselves, their partners, and their families, stressing that physical, social, and emotional maturity are healthier goals than teenage sexual activity.

3. Tell your teenage kids what your views are about sex, even if they don't particularly want to know.

4. Let kids know that being sexual has its hurtful aspects.

5. Remember that your kids may be embarrassed about confronting sexual issues and so may you, but you're better embarrassed than sorry you didn't say what was on your mind.

These guidelines were not for everybody to blindly accept and follow. They were offered as an example for individual parents to modify for their own use. We need to talk to each other candidly, as caring adults, about the limits we set for our children. Faced with a culture that has changed since we grew up, we need to decide what we believe and what we will live with. And we may want to accomplish that in cooperation with other adults in our community who will actively support our conclusions.

Children, even teenagers, need our protection. When we set limits, we are not merely curbing their freedom of choice (although, of course, we are doing that), but we are making decisions about their welfare. Sometimes we are wrong. Sometimes we're too restrictive. Sometimes we're too loose. But within the limits of our own life experience, we parents make judgments that we hope will protect our children from their lack of experience.

Sarah has a thirteen-year-old son named Seth who is six feet tall. Girls of all ages have been hanging around him and Sarah believes Seth has had sexual intercourse with some of them. Sarah told us, "I look at Seth and see a full-grown man and I feel overwhelmed by him. I know I must remember he is still a child and not mature enough for sex, but I haven't been able to talk to him."

Our child's physical development may trick and intimidate us. We forget to talk to the child inside the outer shell of maturity. That child hides behind the false bravado of drugs and alcohol, an abuse which often leads to irresponsible and uncaring sex. The physiological changes of adolescence create enough turmoil without the false liberation of impulses by mind-altering substances. With the help of drugs, young people act on their sexual fantasies and feelings, often in hurtful ways. Boys take on the aura of male conquest, while girls fulfill the desire for care and protection by having a man, fantasies that fit the old stereotypical view of macho men and subservient women.

When a society cannot agree on what is age-appropriate sexual behavior, when no limits or values are expressed, then sexual behavior becomes a personal choice from the smorgasbord of life. The cheapest and easiest values prevail. Sex becomes sensational and children become sex objects.

A young man we know worked as a counselor at a summer camp where he was surprised to find that the twelve-year-olds in his charge were masturbating together openly, sitting around in a "circle jerk." Discussing the issue with other counselors, he found that circle jerks were occurring in every cabin and some counselors felt as uncomfortable as he did, while some found it humorous. But the prevailing attitude was that since the kids weren't hurting anyone, it wasn't the counselors' business. The young man did nothing until one afternoon he came out of the shower and found that a boy had been looking at him and masturbating. He let the boy know, in no uncertain terms, that his behavior was not permissible. He also let his bunk know that masturbation was a private matter.

Neither masturbation nor "circle jerks" are new

phenomena. What is new is our hesitance about what constitutes appropriate sexual behavior and what doesn't. For most of the counselors, the choice was a personal one, left up to each *twelve-year-old* camper. The young man we know set limits based on his own discomfort with the situation. But the incident clearly reflects our culture's confusion with sexual limits. Does letting sex out of the closet mean that we should parade it down Main Street? What's wrong with these young boys masturbating together? Maybe they'll be less inhibited about their sexuality with other men. Or maybe they'll cheer on a rapist, like at the New Bedford gang rape incident.

Parents used to have the greatest say in their children's sexual values, but today's children are influenced by a variety of sources. Not only television, movies, magazines, and other media, but government and private agencies intervene in matters of sexuality. Schools and organizations like Planned Parenthood provide important information and services. Sex education, body care, contraceptive information, and abortion information and counseling are available to young people under eighteen.

The issue of confidentiality for young people under eighteen is a difficult one. Agencies such as Planned Parenthood encourage teenagers to develop their own secrets apart from the family. There is power in having secrets. Such confidentiality, supported by the power of government agencies, suggests that kids are at least their parents' equals and this is a big step into the adult world. While it may be a sign of responsibility for a kid to go to an agency for competent help, how responsible and adult is it really? Neither the agency nor the kid assumes legal or financial responsibility. If the teenager decides to have a child or an abortion with the help of the agency, the young person does not become a ward of

the agency. The agency does not support the new
mother and infant, does not help them manage their
lives, does not supply medical care. Parents are still
responsible. Yet many parents feel that the agencies
collude with their child and assume an almost adver-
sarial position against them.

> I'm so angry and hurt and I don't know
> what to do. My fourteen-year-old daughter Nina
> got involved with some twenty-year-old bum. I
> tried to get the police and counselors to help,
> but nothing seemed to work.
> I just came from a meeting at the Children
> and Youth Agency, where they told me Nina
> went to Planned Parenthood and found out she
> was pregnant. Nina wants to keep her baby and
> now they want to know what we are going to do.
> My husband and I have worked hard to
> raise our family and we were looking forward to
> grandchildren, but Nina's too young. We will
> have to raise another child. I only hope I won't
> blame the kid. I think I need someone who is on
> my side.

But the way things are right now, agencies and
our pop psychological culture see kids and parents
as adversaries, with kids being the victims of their
parents' bad parenting. Many schools, police, courts,
counselors, and other youth-serving agencies still see
parents as the guys with the black hats and view
themselves as wearing the good-guy white hats. There
are some changes occurring. Planned Parenthood,
for instance, is working with the parents of teenagers
now.

On the other side of the issue, the so-called
"Right-to-Lifers" and the Moral Majority folks want
to influence legislation to support their views of right

and wrong. The Moral Majority wants to lead us back to the good old days and stuff sex back in the closet. The "Right-to-Lifers" want to end abortion and return control of a woman's body and her pregnancy to the government. To be effective, moral standards should represent the shared values of the community, the actual beliefs and life-styles of its citizenry.

We are a divergent population from different backgrounds. Nonetheless, we need to come together on common ground and establish clear limits and ethical guidelines for those issues in which we largely concur. We nearly all can agree that abortion should not be a form of birth control, that incest is not a healthy sexual activity, that sex with little children is rape, that rape is an intolerable act of violence. Though all of these abuses have increased in recent years, we cannot afford despair.

As awareness is increased, we can focus on changing current practices which seem to support or encourage abuses. The occurrence of rape, for instance, has increased, but so have efforts to deal with it. Rape victims are beginning to find a more sympathetic environment in the justice system, groups such as Women Organized Against Rape counsel and assist victims, and more rapists are successfully convicted and imprisoned. TOUGHLOVE parents confront these issues in their own families, especially when sexual abuses occur among their children. Patterns like growing up too fast, abusing drugs and alcohol, and taking on adult behavior without adult responsibility are related to inappropriate sexuality and may be successfully challenged by parents and other adults.

I have a good friend who has two daughters and the one daughter (twelve years old) is beginning to mature sexually and I'm worried about her. She is well-behaved, goes to school, gets good grades, and is normal in every respect—except for wearing seductive clothing and acting overly sexy and flirtatious. I feel if she continues this kind of behavior, she will end up being promiscuous at an early age. Could you send me some advice on how her mother can deal with this problem? Also myself? She acts that way even to me. I'm worried that she is going to be that way to the wrong person someday (soon) and will end up either pregnant, raped, or mentally unstable. I would like to know of any TOUGHLOVE groups in my area so I can talk to someone in person. I myself am only twenty-three and well aware of the pressures society is putting on young people nowadays about sex and I am sorry I was initiated (intimidated) into it at the vulnerable age of fifteen. Please send any advice you can.

This woman is the kind of friend we all need. Not many people take the time to worry about someone else's daughter or—much more significantly—to take action on her behalf. Probably this twelve-year-old girl needs to hear how others see her. She may also need to be reassured that she can just be a kid and doesn't need to be sexual now.

There are times when we as parents have to change and learn to tolerate sexual values in our children that we personally find uncomfortable, simply because we want to continue having relationships with them. But we do not have to tolerate those values without qualification or condition. We have our own needs, rights, and preferences as well. What's tough is facing our feelings and emotions when confronted by the sexuality of our own children.

"I opened the door to my bedroom and almost wet my pants when I seen my seventeen-year-old daughter in my bed with her boyfriend." His face was red and he was angry as he spoke. A widower, he had been raising his two children alone for the past three years.

"I didn't move from the door. I yelled at them, 'Get the hell out of my bed! You get upstairs and you, guy, get dressed and get out!' There was my kid stark naked with the cover up to her nose looking scared out of her wits. The guy got his head covered by the sheet. I bet my kid figured I'd clobber them."

He paused, took a deep breath, and smiled.

"I would have a year ago. I'm a hitter from way back. But I learned a lot this past year."

His face darkened as he continued with his story. "After my wife died I see my kids are running wild. My daughter's fifteen then and she stays out. She does bad in school. One night she comes home drunk and I wind up punching her in the face. I give her a black eye. She goes to school and reports me to the nurse and the next thing that I know is this here social worker comes to the house. We really get into it, she wants to take the kids, the girl wants to go, sort of, and her brother's crying. It comes out how bad she is and I'm at my wits' end.

"This social worker agrees not to take the kids and we go for counseling. After a few sessions she says she wants me to go to a TOUGHLOVE meeting and she takes me there. I've been going there ever since and I don't hit no more and the kids are a lot better.

"The girl goes to school, gets good grades, and comes home on time. She likes some of the parents in my group and even goes places with me sometimes.

"So when I see this scene before my eyes, I want to kill her and the SOB. But instead I walk to my telephone and call my TOUGHLOVE buddy and we talk and talk. I can hear her upstairs crying.

"Well, later I go up and tell the kid that I want to talk to her and her boyfriend. She doesn't want to call him and cries a lot. Finally she does and he comes over all hangdog, looking at the floor.

"I sit down and tell them that if they're old enough for sex, then they're old enough to take responsibility for what they're doing. I give them a lecture on sex and caring and consideration for each other and that it's not just a lark and people get hurt—bodies and feelings. I hope they understand that and above all to stay the hell out of my room and my house with their sex life. I add that they've taken on adult responsibilities now and part of that includes being thoughtful of me.

"All the time I'm saying these words I went over and over with my TOUGHLOVE buddy on the phone, I'm thinking, 'What the hell am I talking about? They've been going together for a year and probably screwing their brains out,' but I don't say it. 'I don't bring women home,' I say and 'Buddy, you better be using protection.'

"All the kids do is stare at me. My daughter says, 'Oh, Daddy, how stupid do you think we are?' 'Not stupid, kid, just careless.' I said everything I got to say and end with telling them to stay out of my room.

"You want to know something?" he says with his smile returning. "This here kid, my daughter, kisses me and the jerk holds out his hand and shakes hands with me."

The sexual choices our kids make have all kinds of repercussions. Our desire to have a close family forces us to accept sexuality in ways we had not envisaged. Our old attitudes and values have been blown wide open and new family structures and ways of being sexual have emerged. Recently, we went to a baby shower given for a woman who had been artificially inseminated to produce a female child. The woman and her mate are both lesbians, both in their late thirties, well-educated, and responsible. What a different family this will be. What will they tell the child about her lineage? How will they protect her from the hurts that will surely come as others discover her heritage? Will the society-at-large support this family beyond its narrow and unusual framework?

Technological advance brings us wider choice, which challenges our narrow thinking and feeling. Old values and myths conflict with new situations as people choose children from sperm banks, select the sex of their child, transfer embryos from one womb to another, and fix problems "in utero." When an abusive kid screams at his parent, "I didn't ask to be born," the parent knows that it is more true than ever before.

A good friend of ours half-joked recently that she is no longer a liberal. Her twenty-three-year-old daughter informed her that she was a lesbian and the news shocked her right "out of her tolerance." She always knew she could accept someone else's child's being gay, but her own kid's revelation put her in a tailspin. "What's wrong with me?" she said. Right now our friend is busy gathering support for herself so she can come to terms with her feelings and responses.

Another parent came to a TOUGHLOVE group asking help in changing her son's sexuality. She and her husband were upset that he was gay. Some group members said to get him to a psychiatrist, others suggested family counseling, until someone asked the mother about other aspects of her son's life. She said that he was twenty-seven, had a master's degree, was a practicing engineer, made a good living, and lived in a nice apartment. Obviously he was not an acting-out kid but an adult who chose to be gay and was taking responsibility for his own life and life-style.

A young woman in the group then spoke up. "My brother is gay and I love him. It's not anybody's fault. It's just what he is." Other group members assured the woman that it was not a fault for her son to be gay, that she did not have to be ashamed, that it's an option people are taking today, and maybe it's not so bad. The woman expressed appreciation for the group's understanding and support.

The group helped the parents stop grieving over the loss of their child as they had imagined he would be and recognize the person their child has become. Some parents cannot bear to have a homosexual child, others can. These folks gradually decided their son was not crazy and that they were not bad people. They accepted their son's sexual choice. The group helped these parents speak about their feelings toward their son and helped him recognize how difficult his sexual choice was for his parents to accept, even though they loved him without rejecting him. Their acceptance and decision to have a relationship with him meant a lot of work for the family. Group members helped them work out answers to questions like "How do I treat my son's lovers? Do they sleep together in my home? Do I talk to my relatives about my son? What does he want me to tell the family?" Their son had to answer questions like "Who do I bring home? How can I respect their wishes with respect to the rest of the family and friends? What do I do with my feeling that I should be instantly accepted?"

Still another woman reluctantly told her TOUGH-LOVE group that she herself was a lesbian and that her son blackmailed her with that information, using her fear of exposure to perpetuate his druggie life-style. When she took the difficult risk of telling her group, she ended his blackmail. She was out of the closet and still accepted by her group.

"What do you do when your daughter's twenty and comes home and tells you she's chosen to be a single parent and doesn't want a husband?" asked Mya. "I see myself as thoroughly modern about these ideas for other people, but all I could say was 'How can you make life so hard for yourself?' I felt angry and betrayed, especially since she told me long after the fact."

It's a whole new ball game for most people when the crisis is theirs: when it's their kid, their family, and they have to face these major issues. No matter what choices are made, emotions, ideas, thoughts, values, and relationships undergo change as the family reassesses itself and seeks a new balance.

Mya considers herself a modern liberal woman who believes in the rights of the individual, in choice, in freedom, but also in family and education. She feels support and community is a necessity for human growth. She and her husband, Larry, have survived many storms in their twenty-four years of marriage. Larry is a journalist, Mya works in a health food store. They are creative, artistic people who are into health foods, even helping their TOUGHLOVE group to raise money with a natural food bake sale. They are thoughtful people, involved in ecology, community, and child-rearing. After raising their kids, they now look forward to being with each other. They came to TOUGHLOVE because their youngest daughter, Gemma, was in trouble with drugs. After they took some firm stands and developed a support network, things began to straighten out. Gemma went off to college and was now living at home temporarily, having taken a semester off from college.

One day Gemma announced to her parents, "I'm

pregnant." Mya and Larry were not too surprised by this announcement, since they had had many discussions about birth control with Gemma and never were reassured as to her use of it. She always said, "Don't worry, I won't get pregnant. And if I do, it's my problem." They always replied, "Use birth control. We will not live with a baby." Although Larry and Mya believed in the choice of abortion, they did not approve of abortion as birth control.

Gemma made her announcement and she was close to tears, but she looked pretty belligerent. Mya felt a flood of anger and sympathy for her daughter, but she didn't want another crisis. She felt selfish.

"Who's the father?" Larry asked. "And what do you intend to do?"

"It doesn't matter who. He doesn't want me anyway," she cried and ran from the room. They followed her into the next room. "He rejected me," she said and in their hearts they knew who he was, an old love that Gemma had been holding on to, and again they felt anger and empathy for her.

Did she want to get pregnant? The old question rose in them—didn't she care about herself? Did she plan this? Is this her rebellion? Mya wanted to hold her daughter to her and wanted to kill her at the same time. She did hold her, but spoke more harshly than she liked and tears rolled down her face.

Larry stood at the door looking on. He wanted her to confess who the father was, but didn't say so. Instead he said things like, "Yes, it's painful, but what are you going to do? How far along are you? Have you been to a doctor?" She responded, "Two months, I think. I did the pregnancy test. No, I didn't go to a doctor."

Larry insisted that she go to a doctor. He offered to make the appointment, but she resisted. It took some time, but finally she made the appointment and confirmed the pregnancy.

"I know you want me to get an abortion, but I'm not. I want this baby."

Mya and Larry talked to Gemma about the difficulty of raising a child alone, of the future, of telling her child about his or her father. They tried to push back Gemma's defiance, but only made her more defensive. She told them that she was going to have the baby no matter what. She had some friends who supported her in her decision and finally her parents came to accept that she would have the baby.

When Mya and Larry accepted the inevitability of their daughter's motherhood, they fell quiet and thoughtful. They looked at themselves, their lives and limits, their feelings. They turned to TOUGH-LOVE friends to help them sort things out. Their dreams never included their child as a parent without a partner. They felt their grandchild would have a strike against him or her already, without a father.

Their feelings ranged between sadness and fear for their daughter and her unborn child. They felt hatred toward the likely father. They were willing to support their daughter emotionally and physically, but were not willing to live with a baby in their house.

Mya asked Gemma to go to a counselor to get some help in sorting out her own head. Gemma had a job to which she could bring her baby, but she had to work out those arrangements and begin to save money. Larry and Mya had a hard time doing it, but they gave her a deadline for moving out because they wanted her in her own place when she had the baby. A woman friend of the family took Gemma to lunch and told her that if she couldn't find a place, Gemma could stay with her. Gemma's best friend, married with children of her own, offered to coach her through childbirth. Finally, she did find a small place she could afford and, with her parents' help, she moved in.

Larry and Mya's TOUGHLOVE friends helped them limit their tendency to be too generous. They assisted their daughter financially, but offered no frills. Her friends at work gave her a shower and she was ready when the baby came, a fine little girl.

Gemma's family has had to face many questions and feelings. Her sister, Betsy, felt disgust, shame, anger, and embarrassment, all at the same time. She felt mean for being so hurt and hurtful. Other TOUGHLOVE people helped Betsy with her feelings, since Mya and Larry were steeped in their own ambivalent feelings. Both family and friends got angry at Gemma for allowing the baby's father in and out of her life. Mya and Larry made appointments to see Gemma and the baby, so that they would not accidentally meet him at her home. Friends helped Mya curb her extravagance toward the baby.

Because family ties are so important to them and because they are baby Liza's only grandparents, Mya and Larry feel even more strongly about the importance of being a family to Gemma and Liza. Mya says that it makes her feel protective toward both daughter and granddaughter, more responsible. But Gemma, debating about how to bring Liza up, lets Mya know that "This is my baby." Mya is sure her relationship to this baby is colored by its beginning and that Larry and she will feel differently toward Liza than toward other grandchildren in traditional families.

Visiting cousin Michael, six years old, says "Where's Liza's daddy? I don't understand how a lady can have a baby without a daddy. You have to be married." Gemma laughs and says that she's not married and the baby's daddy doesn't live with her. Michael walks away shaking his head. We tell little kids that people get married and have babies, no matter how modern we think we are.

Mya and Larry wonder how little Liza will feel and be treated while growing up. They hope that the culture will become more accepting. They are sure that if Gemma had been fourteen or fifteen, they would have insisted on an abortion.

But most of all, they're surprised at the upheaval in their lives brought about by their daughter's personal decisions. They could easily accept the decision of a twenty-two-year-old, even if they might not agree with it, but when it's their own kid, no matter how old, it's hard.

We all want our children to have it easier, to give them the good life. If they'd only take it. We forget people have to earn their own good life.

Larry and Mya are still surprised at their own values. They realized that they wanted their daughter to have an abortion because they really favored the traditional family situation. "Don't have kids while you're single. Get a future before you have kids. Only be a single parent if you're in your thirties." Sorting out old and new values isn't easy. Mya and Larry wonder how Gemma's life will go and how she'll see this part of her life later on. Certainly she has made a lifelong commitment.

The sexual choices our children make have repercussions that challenge us and our values. We are torn between our desire for a close, loving family and behavior in our children that we don't like. Yet families have to deal with their conflicts, the feelings, and the issues and TOUGHLOVE helps them along the way.

CHAPTER 7:

Parent Abuse

ABC News recently reported a study which indicates that one and a half million kids will physically attack their parents, grandparents, or siblings this year by pushing, hitting, beating with fists, sticks, bats, stabbing with knives, or shooting with guns. According to this study, a child born in 1970 is three times more likely to do violence to a member of his family than someone born in 1950.

Help!! I'm sitting here watching the television and everything you are saying is like it's coming out of my own mouth (or at least my heart). My son Jerry is very young (ten years old). He has been kicked out of five different schools for punching other children and for attacking teachers. He is uncontrollable at home. He lives only for himself. There is no respect for us. He's only nice when he wants something. Everything out of his mouth is disrespectful. Dirty looks are always on his face. I'm suffering chronic depression because of his behavior.

His father sent him to my husband and I because he couldn't handle him. Now it's all up to us. I'm so worried that if we don't get the *right* help now, that he'll end up in serious trouble.

The doctor here has him on Ritalin for hyperactivity, but now Jerry thinks that "little pill" is the answer and that he doesn't need to change himself! What if he grows up feeling a pill will cure all? Every social worker or counselor we've been to *always* puts it *on my head* that my first bad marriage is to blame, that I've been a bad parent and now I have to pay! We're at the point of putting him in a foster home or juvenile hall. But I love him and so does his stepfather. . . . Your "Parents are boss" and "Good behavior for room and board" are just how we feel. . . .

You're our last resort. We live in a small city, but please write back *soon*. Let me know where to go!! Our whole family is on the line. We love Jerry, but if he doesn't cool it, we're going to put him away. I know you may not think a ten-year-old could be that bad, but believe me, I wouldn't write you if I wasn't desperate.

Help us! Please write soon!

Jerry's parents were referred to a nearby parent support group. The group told them to put away their guilt about their divorce and the possible trauma that Jerry experienced. Later on, when Jerry was under control, the family could resolve that psychological issue if it was still important.

The first action step Jerry's parents took, with the support of the group members, was to develop a new approach for Jerry at school. Although he had been assigned to a male teacher who was able to restrain him when he acted out, he still tested that situation often, carrying on for as long as an hour and pushing the teacher's patience to the limit.

The next time Jerry started to punch some kids at recess, the teacher restrained him and sent a message to the office. Within ten minutes, several TOUGHLOVE parents arrived and took over the task of restraining Jerry, who was still storming. They told him that they would not turn him loose until he stopped his bad behavior. After an hour he finally settled down and the parents left.

The second school incident occurred after Jerry was reprimanded for loud talking. He shouted and ran around the classroom, but this time it took only ten minutes for the TOUGHLOVE parents to settle him down. Since then his school behavior has been more manageable and he is still in the same school after a year. He has an occasional tantrum, but gets himself under control when the teacher takes a firm stand with him.

The problem at home was treated in much the same way, except Jerry's stepfather agreed to take the primary responsibility for dealing with the boy, while his mother agreed to back off. In our experience we have found that the stepparent usually has a more realistic view of the situation than the biological parent. But backing off is not easy to do and a parent often needs support from group members just to remain aloof. Jerry's mother needed a lot of help with this, so support parents came over to the house to take her outside while her husband and the other parents restrained Jerry. They chided her about being more difficult than her son.

Jerry did become more manageable with the support group's intervention. But without the help of other parents, Jerry did not seem able to stop himself once he got going. One day Jerry came home from school in one of his moods and seemed like he was working himself up to a full-blown tantrum. After supper, when he was asked to help with the dishes, he started breaking them.

Mom and Dad, without thinking, each grabbed him and held him. They told him that they were sick of his behavior and that he couldn't behave that way at home. They told him he could not use hyperactivity or his parents' divorce as excuses for his behavior. Mom and Dad (they had decided that Jerry's stepfather was Dad whether Jerry liked it or not) would not allow him to behave like a big spoiled two-year-old.

"When my husband and I held Jerry down, I finally realized what it meant when you say 'Parents are boss.' The nice thing about it is Jerry realized it too. He is almost becoming a pleasure to live with and we are working with his doctor to eliminate the medication."

Violent behavior is certainly not limited to boys:

I just finished reading an article about TOUGHLOVE. It sure seems to hit home.

We've had problems with our oldest daughter, who will be thirteen soon. There are times I think we're making progress and then again I wonder.

If she doesn't get her way, she thinks all she has to do is start beating or threatening her younger brother. It is getting out of hand more and more often. She's big for her age and it's getting so I'm also getting to be one of her victims. I really feel if we don't do something now, things are really going to get worse.

Do you have any TOUGHLOVE groups in this area? If not, could I possibly somehow get a manual of yours? I'd appreciate any help you can give me.

We referred the mother to a TOUGHLOVE group and the solution was an innovative approach to dealing with acting-out teen girls. Another family in the group also had a thirteen-year-old who was the prime problem in their brood of eight children. They traded daughters.

The girl from the family of four was lost in the hubbub of a large family and annoyed by the logistical problems of feeding, bathing, and getting off to school with all those kids around. There was little privacy and none of the kids had his or her own bedroom.

The other girl missed the action in a busy household. She quickly found the quiet life of a small family boring and was as anxious as the other daughter to negotiate a way back to her own home.

Each set of parents, with their support people, developed a set of conditions for living which were accepted by their respective daughters. The contracts were reviewed weekly until everyone felt that the situation had been adequately resolved.

Said one of the mothers, "My daughter made an interesting comment recently. She told me that even though we were not like the Walton family on TV, she liked us better. I think living somewhere else for just a week helped the kids separate dream from reality. I think she found out that living happily ever after is something you have to work at and not even parents can give it to you."

Creative solutions, like the families trading daughters, do not always work. But they are better than doing nothing and certainly more interesting. Besides, they shake things up and let kids know that changes are in the making.

A very proper lady at one of our Weekend Workshops struggled with telling us her story because she was uncomfortable even spelling the words her daughter used. "When she is angry at me, she curses and uses the *f* word" was the closest she could get to expressing her daughter's abusive language. The audience made a number of suggestions, but the woman only agreed to think about the situation further, read the manual, and report back to the group on the second day of the workshop.

Instead, she went home and was preparing dinner when her daughter came into the kitchen. "Oh, are we having that fucking shit for dinner again?" muttered the teen.

With spontaneous rage, her mother whirled around and screamed at the top of her lungs, "If you don't like the fucking food, then you can make your own fucking dinner!"

Her daughter was stunned. She responded very timidly, "Well, I'm sorry. But you don't have to talk to me with that kind of language."

The mother laughingly reported to the other workshop participants the next day, "And I didn't have a bit of trouble with her the rest of the evening."

No miracle cure, of course, but a dramatic change in a parent's way of responding can be a catalyst for further change. Refusing to accept verbal and physical abuse is an important step and it helps to be creative about the way you show your refusal. With the kind of kids we're talking about, parents have little to lose by trying the unusual and the humorous.

Brainstorming creative solutions can also be fun. Many practical solutions arise from humorous suggestions. In dealing with verbal abuse from kids, we have heard of solutions like: using obscene language in front of the kid's friends to give them a taste of how it feels when they use inappropriate language around a parent's friends, taping their abusive language and playing it on a stereo as loud as the kid plays rock music, or opening the windows wide when a kid uses abusive language so that he or she is embarrassed by going public in the neighborhood.

Another single mom, Lucille, came to TOUGH-LOVE because her three large sons had reached the point where they simply didn't listen to her. Lucille is a lawyer and a self-confident person who always had good discipline with her kids. But she began to find her authority challenged.

One day she told her sixteen-year-old, Jay, that he could not go out until he'd mowed the lawn and done his homework. He agreed. But when the weekend came, Jay had done neither his chores nor his schoolwork, so she reminded him of his agreement. He did nothing about it.

On Saturday night Jay got dressed to go out and Lucille told him, "Jay, I warned you to get your work finished. You're not going out."

"But Ma, I've got tickets to the concert and I'm going. I'll do the lawn tomorrow."

"Nothing doing. You're grounded. Stay home and finish your schoolwork and do the lawn tomorrow."

Just then Mason, eighteen, and Terry, fifteen, came downstairs and announced that they were going to the concert too. "We're going, Mom, and there's nothing you can do about it."

Lucille looked aghast as her three large sons walked by her and out the door. She felt as if she had just been smacked across the face.

"Get back here right now," she shouted after them.

"Sorry, Ma, we don't have to listen to you anymore." And they left.

She was shocked. She sat down on the sofa and

shook her head. Picking up the telephone, she called some friends and told them what had happened.

"I don't know. Maybe they're right," said one friend. "Maybe you just have to let go." But that didn't sound right to her.

"You need a man around," said another.

The next day, Sunday, the boys acted as if nothing had happened. Everything was peaches and cream and the lawn got mowed. Lucille didn't say anything either, but this was the beginning of what was to become an established pattern of her sons coming and going as they pleased, doing chores when or if they pleased, and Lucille feeling like a boarder in her own home.

Lucille came to TOUGHLOVE about one year later. Her youngest son, Terry, had been drunk on two consecutive evenings. She also found her oldest son, Mason, half-dressed with his girlfriend in his room. When he waved hello to her, she became furious and demanded that the girl leave. He told the girl to stay. Lucille raised her hand to smack him and he grabbed her arm and pushed her against the wall. He told her to shut up, that this was his home too. Then he let her go and closed his door. Lucille cried, left the house, and drove around all night— determined to do something, but not sure what.

One Friday evening a few weeks later, Lucille called her sons into the living room. She asked them to sit down.

"You boys have been torturing me with the way you've been acting. Things are going to change. Jay, you are failing school, I think you steal money, and you are totally abusive to me. On Monday you're going to school and you're going to start straightening out. And I won't tolerate your back talk anymore. Terry, you're a drunk and on Monday you're getting help for your drinking problem. And you,

Mason, are a bully and a doper. You're leaving home until you get yourself some help with your dope and change your attitude."

The boys' looks of surprise began to fade and they started to leave, laughing and cursing at their mother's outburst. Suddenly four very large men walked into the living room.

"Hello," said one man to the three stunned boys. "My name is Alan. We're here to help your mother out tonight and we'll be here whenever she needs us. We're all very concerned about what kind of people you're becoming and the way you bully your mother."

Lucille nodded and spoke. "Terry and Jay, go upstairs and pack your bags. Alan and his wife have agreed to have you stay at their house this weekend."

Alan motioned to the two boys and he and one of the other men escorted them upstairs.

"Mason," said another, "my name is Carl and this is Bill. Come on out on the porch. We're going to have a little talk."

Mason shrugged. Lucille thought he might be afraid that they were going to beat him up, but he went with them. The others came downstairs and Lucille was told they had agreed to spend the weekend at Alan's.

"Don't worry about a thing," Alan assured her. "Jay will be at the meeting you scheduled at school on Monday and we'll see that Terry gets to the interview at the rehab."

They left and Carl and Bill came in with Mason.

Carl said, "Mason hasn't made up his mind what he wants to do. He understands that he can't stay here until he's made some changes, but he's not sure what to do next. The three of us are going over to the diner to get something to eat and to talk things over some more. Give my wife a call if you need anything or if you just want to talk."

He patted her on the arm and smiled reassuringly. Lucille watched as the two men left with her sons and then she sat down and cried with relief. It had gone smoother than she expected. Although her anxiety continued throughout the weekend, the telephone calls from parents in her TOUGHLOVE group helped her a lot.

By Monday afternoon the situation had been structured for each of the boys. Terry, the drinker, had been admitted to an inpatient drug and alcohol abuse program for ninety days. Jay, in the meeting with the assistant principal, had agreed to attend school and classes faithfully and get tutoring in his two worst subjects. With his teachers turning in weekly progress reports, TOUGHLOVE parents would check on his attendance, his homework, and whether he got home from school promptly, observed curfew, and did his chores.

Mason decided not to come home and he went to live with his girlfriend's family. Lucille was not pleased with his choice, but assured him that he could come home whenever he was ready to clean up his act. She explained herself to the girlfriend's mother and father and invited them to a TOUGHLOVE meeting. So far they haven't come to one, but they're not unfriendly to her.

Terry, after returning from a successful experience at the rehab, and Jay have been doing well. The close monitoring of schoolwork, chores, and curfews has become very casual and the boys have nice relationships with the men who helped supervise them. And Lucille is in charge of her family and her home again.

Not just single parents but elderly parents may need help dealing with physical intimidation:

> I am so ashamed to be writing this letter, but I don't know what to do. I am sixty-eight

and my wife is sixty-two. We have two wonderful children: one is a teacher and our daughter is married to a fine young man and busy raising her own family. They both live on the West Coast now.

I don't know what went wrong with our youngest son, aged twenty-six. He went off to college, but dropped out. Two years ago he returned home because of a nervous breakdown. We had him hospitalized, but he never seemed to get better. He lives at home with us and attends the outpatient clinic. He says he can't work, sleeps all day, and goes out to bars all night.

Lately he has been bringing people home against our wishes. He has pushed us into our bedroom and put a large dresser against the door. My wife and I are afraid for our lives, but the hospital says my son is getting better. I can't put my son out because we are all he has, but things are getting worse. He has made us black and blue by his rough handling. Can you tell us how to save our son?

We have occasionally received letters from elderly folks who are almost prisoners in their own homes. We urge them to take several steps, but first and foremost we urge them to join a parent support group. Then, with support along the way, they can contact the police, obtain a restraining order, and inform the hospital outpatient clinic about what's really going on at home. When that son returned home one evening, he found a living room full of large men waiting to escort him and his belongings away from his parents' home or to an inpatient alcoholism program. Ideally, not only TOUGHLOVE group members are involved but neighbors as well, so that the parents have immediate support should their son try to return home. On more than one occasion young people we know, when confronted by such a choice, have entered a rehab or treatment program.

We caution TOUGHLOVE groups from taking such an overt action too readily. Although group members may be concerned about the parents' well-being, they may also find that the young man moves back home without any consequences. In these instances Mom and Dad were not committed to the action and needed a less drastic bottom line and plan.

Getting the police involved and getting a re-straining order may be a less dramatic and more realistic step for parents to agree to and will provide the parents with some legal protection from their abusive offspring. Parents, particularly those acting on their own, have reported some difficulty in getting cooperation from the police. "They said it was a domestic squabble and that they don't get involved in domestic situations" is the complaint that we have often heard from angry parents. Policemen we have talked with explain that more cops are killed or injured in so-called domestic squabbles than in any other kind of situation. Ironically, a policeman may end up in the hospital while the family members reconcile and decide not to press charges against each other.

Certainly not all police departments will indicate such reluctance, but that is where a restraining or-der, protection from abuse order, or peace bond comes in handy. Although the name of the legal device and the procedure vary from state to state, parents may obtain legal protection from a court which formally names their son or daughter as *likely to do violence* to someone in the household and provides police with a clearly defined situation that they must respond to. Parents are, in effect, pressing charges in advance of a possible incident so that they can get help quickly when they need it and so that their violent child knows that his or her behavior is now a matter of public record. Young people are usually shocked to find that their parents have mobilized the law to protect them, a response quite different than they expect.

What is helpful to parents in seeking such legal protection and to other parents hoping to obtain the support and assistance of county agencies for other purposes is a written chronology of the problems that they have had with their son or daughter. It is much easier to get backing from judges, probation officers, and caseworkers when they see a long history of abuse by a child and efforts by parents to cope with that abuse, particularly if it is presented in writing.

Some situations are grim and frightening, such as the following:

> My mother-in-law has a really bad problem with her seventeen-year-old. He came home one night and kept her sitting on the couch by pointing a .357 Magnum at her. He wound up shooting himself in the leg, but didn't realize it because he was so high. He has beat her up several times, but she is afraid for her life and won't tell on him.
>
> We live too far away to help and my husband tries to talk to his brother on the phone, but he won't listen. Can you help? Everyone in our family is going crazy with worry.

The solution here is clear. Immediately notify the police, seek support for the mother-in-law with the nearest TOUGHLOVE group and neighbors, get all guns out of the house, and get her out of the house during these confrontations. This is not a time for innovation. Guns kill. Drugs and guns kill more readily. A person's life is in jeopardy. The police will respond to such situations—even if it's a family squabble. Take action promptly.

In the 1983 study cited by ABC News, some very discouraging news accompanied the startling estimate of a million and a half acts of violence toward family members by kids this year. A psychiatrist reported that 50 percent of today's violent kids can't be helped and unless they somehow learn to control themselves they would end up in prison. Three quarters of a million new prison inmates in the next few years. Can we afford such waste? Or are there solutions?

We're going to have to think more clearly. No more slipshod psychologizing. Like on a recent "Donahue" program which purported to focus on the issue of "parent abuse." Instead, the conversation drifted into blaming parents for their violent children—equating parents who spanked their young children with teenagers brutalizing their families. The show closed with a teenage boy who had physically abused his mother lecturing the audience on how they should raise their children. The young man implied that if his mother had communicated with him, he wouldn't have beaten her up. Never mind the facts, just pack the show with controversy.

This "Donahue" show demonstrated exactly those pop psychological attitudes that excuse, reinforce, and support violent behavior. We can all think of experiences in our lives that could justify violence. Gandhi, Martin Luther King, Jr., and Jesus Christ had reasons to be violent. But excusing people's violent behavior gives it tacit approval, a kind of thinking exemplified by the implication of "What can you expect from your son? You spanked him."

To all this, TOUGHLOVE says "Baloney." There are no excuses for violence. We need to confront violent behavior in ways that let young people and adults know it is not acceptable. To do this we need the help and support of other adults in our community. We cannot afford to wring our hands. We can find solutions.

CHAPTER 8:

Suicide

Young people we know who have been suicidal are not, as popular belief would have it, suffering long-standing depression. Rather they are mostly unrealistic, having expectations greater than life is likely to fulfill. They are kids who like to escape, through fantasy, through drugs, and through alcohol. They live in their dreams with their wishes, expecting unconditional love and wanting someone to take care of them, to solve their problems for them over and over again.

They say things like "I felt lost." Or "I wanted them to feel sorry." Or "I thought it was easier." Or "I felt that everyone hated me and wanted me to die."

Their reasons include being upset by moving to a new neighborhood, their parents' divorce, a parent's death, or a parent's alcoholism. They are upset by being rich, or poor, or middle-class, or fat, or skinny, or crippled, or too short, or too tall.

They have grown up in a culture which suggests

that life can be lived without pain. There are pills for physical suffering and pills for mental suffering as well. Learning how to cope with life's bumps and bruises is one of the skills that young people need for their own independence, but many teens are busily avoiding the whole process, betting on utopia.

There is a time in all of our lives when we recognize that we're alone—individuals in the world. We might describe ourselves as feeling abandoned, rejected, lost, or lonely. We may feel scared, angry, or hurt. We know we are vulnerable and we hate it. We know we have to live our own lives and it scares us, but most of us go out and do it. We seek attachments—like work or religion or family or friends—to fill our inner void.

Adolescence is a time of emptiness, for clearing out the trappings of childhood in preparation for adulthood, for an evolving self that is developing skills and experiencing life. That feeling of emptiness is appropriate for young people in their adolescent years, appropriate for who they are at that time in their life.

But in today's world teenagers and adults are encouraged and urged to "know themselves," to focus on feelings and inadequacies, and to satisfy one's inner needs. The old benchmarks of maturity, based on external criteria like graduation, marriage, and career attainments, have given way to internal, less tangible criteria: desires and expectations, the realization of one's self. As enslaved by conformity to the fantasies of developing and exploring an inner self as we were previously enslaved by conformity to external cultural demands, we pursue a new self that is without structure and forever adolescent.

Adolescents don't have a lot of self outside of their "child self" and what little they have often doesn't seem very real to them. Who they are emerges as they try on different roles, an outer-directed process that helps them fill out who they are. A total focus on inner searching, as suggested by today's culture, leaves people constantly feeling unreal. Our current cultural obsession with feelings has magnified the natural turmoil of adolescence. For many young folks the process of separating from parents means alienating parents, defining one's own space means intruding on others with a blasting stereo or excluding others with stereo headphones, feeling good means getting high, and suicide means a solution to one's problems.

I thought the end of the world had come when we broke up. I thought I couldn't face living without him. I felt so lost I just wanted to die. So I went into the bathroom and cut my wrist and watched the blood go down the sink. I really thought, "He'll be sorry. They'll all be sorry." When they rescued me I was mad. I didn't want to see anyone. My mother's face really broke me up. I didn't want to see her. I wanted to stay mad. After a while on the psychiatric unit, I decided a lot of those other kids were stupid and I thought, "So was I." I gave up and I'm glad I didn't die now.

I can remember planning my own funeral. How beautiful I'd look and everyone would be there. They would say such terrific things, but I can't exactly remember what they were saying, but it was trash like "She was so good"—and how they cried! It just made me cry to think about it. The whole school was there.

Ironically, some troubled young folks get in touch with life when they give up drugs, only to turn toward suicide as another escape route from the reality they now must experience.

It's funny, but while I was doing drugs I didn't give a shit about anyone. My parents didn't even exist, except for being all over me. Even my grandma's crying seemed funny to me. I didn't care. But when I stopped doing dope and I began to feel, I saw how much I hurt everyone.

I felt awful. I felt I was the most evil person in the whole world and I made everyone I loved suffer. So you know what I did? I was so selfish I took a whole handful of downers.

When I woke up and my parents were in the room, I screamed at them and made them leave. I couldn't stand to see how sorry they looked. When they left, I kept holding my head and pulling my hair, but someone stopped me. I don't know what was really going on then. I just think I felt sorry for myself. I felt like I was this great awful creature and everyone hated me.

When I got out, I stayed for a while at this other family's house. That helped a lot. And at first I only would see my dad. Later my therapist, my mother, some TOUGHLOVE parents, and I had a meeting and I told her how much I really cared and I didn't even fall apart, but we cried.

I had to know I could do things on my own, so I didn't go home but moved to Colorado. When I got to my new place, I checked in with a local TOUGHLOVE group. Those people had me to dinner! I lived with a friend I'd known from rehab days and got a job. It wasn't easy.

One never thinks of suicide as humorous, but even the dark side of life can be funny. Consider the absurdity of suicide in this young woman's tale.

I was fat and ugly. My whole family was fat and I hated them and no one liked me or wanted me, so I decided to hang myself. I took the fire rope outside my window and tied it on the chandelier in the dining room. I moved the table and got onto the chair. I kicked the chair and (don't you dare laugh) the light fixture, the ceiling, and me came tumbling down. Well, that proved it. I was even too fat to kill myself.

Right there I went on a diet. But try explaining that chandelier and ceiling to your family. They guessed and were hysterical. I kept saying, "Look I'm alive, I'm OK." But they made me go to a psychologist. It wasn't so bad. He got me into a group with other fat kids and now I'm a little thinner and go out with this guy who's not too skinny either.

P.S. I know this is a sad story, but you have to admit it's funny too. One day I'll write a novel around it.

Some of the TOUGHLOVE groups have become very sophisticated about dealing with suicide. Many group members have attended seminars about suicide and share their knowledge with the others in their group. One TOUGHLOVE group published the following suicide fact sheet for general distribution.

WARNING SIGNS OF SUICIDE

SUICIDE THREATS: Any expression of suicidal thought should be taken seriously. Those who threaten are those who act.
STATEMENTS REVEALING A DESIRE TO DIE: Comments like "I just want it all to end" or "It would be better for everyone if I was gone" are ominous signs.

PREVIOUS SUICIDE ATTEMPTS: Four of five persons who commit suicide have made one or more previous attempts. If someone you know has such a history, be especially attentive.

CHANGES IN BEHAVIOR: Withdrawal, apathy, moodiness, changes in sleep patterns, changes in eating habits, anxiety, gloominess—any of these can be symptoms of developing depression. Lack of concentration and curtailing of social interactions are also warning signs of inner turmoil.

FINAL ARRANGEMENTS: Giving away personal possessions, putting one's things in order, and other signs of expected departure may indicate a suicide plan.

WHAT TO DO

REACH OUT: Let them know you are concerned and want to help.

DISCUSS IT OPENLY AND FRANKLY: Talking about suicide will not encourage a person to try it—quite the contrary, honest, accepting discussion shows that you are willing to understand.

DON'T AVOID THE ISSUE: It may be uncomfortable for you both, but if you show unwillingness to discuss the issue, this may only frustrate the attempt at communication and reinforce the idea that others find the idea and therefore the person repugnant and unacceptable.

GET PROFESSIONAL HELP: Students often feel that professional help is unavailable to them. The following offer twenty-four-hour suicide prevention and crisis assistance:

[local phone numbers were supplied by the group for people to call].

Unfortunately, getting help is not always as simple as calling a hot line. A TOUGHLOVE group brought a girl to a mental health clinic where the psychiatrist insisted that the young woman seemed perfectly rational. Asserting themselves as TOUGHLOVE parents have learned to do, they literally pulled off her slacks and showed the psychiatrist the self-inflicted burns and cuts on her body from previous incidents.

A father and a TOUGHLOVE support person brought his son to a hospital emergency room, unconscious from booze and pills. When the kid revived, he stormed out of the hospital. The doctor said he could do nothing to stop him, since the hospital had no grounds to hold him. Dad knew he needed help, so he called the police and said that a patient had fled the hospital and was "a danger to himself." As a social worker, the father knew that the police would respond to that language. They did and, with the police, his father, and the hospital staff standing there, the boy voluntarily admitted himself to the hospital for further treatment.

Another couple had to sit on their daughter. She had agreed to stay home when her parents grounded her for cutting school. Suddenly, after receiving a telephone call, she changed her mind and insisted on going out. When her folks refused to let her out the door, she ran into the kitchen and began to rub a knife against her wrist. Her father grabbed her, took the knife, and when she quieted down, he released her. She suddenly put her hand through a glass window and threatened to cut herself again. This time her parents wouldn't let her up until the police arrived.

The police escorted the family to the local emergency service and left. The doctor who interviewed the daughter felt she wasn't suicidal, gave her a sedative, and told her parents she needed to do something with her temper. The parents tried to explain their fear, repeated their description of her behavior, and asked if she could be kept for observation. The doctor said he didn't see any reason to keep her, that she was calm and denied any suicidal gesture or attempt. Incredibly, he was prepared to believe the kid over her parents.

They took her home and called parents in the TOUGHLOVE group who insisted on spending the night and helping them watch over their daughter. The next day they found a psychiatrist who dealt with Mom and Dad as responsible adults and their daughter as a potential suicide victim.

Not only kids attempt suicide. Here is a letter from a woman who used TOUGHLOVE to deal with her father.

> My father is a compulsive gambler, which was always a source of shame to my family and a not-too-well-kept family secret. My mother worked hard her whole life, often to pay outstanding debts that my father owed. Through her work she had a wonderful insurance plan, so when she died my father inherited almost $100,000. He quickly gambled the money away and began asking my husband and me for money. I decided not to help support my father's gambling anymore by giving him money.
>
> When I refused to do that, he said he was in a lot of trouble and if he didn't get some cash, he would kill himself. He began to call all of our relatives to say that he was "going away for a while and just wanted to say good-bye." They, of

course, called me to ask if my father was all right. I knew that he was trying to scare me. And he was.

I called a friend from the TOUGHLOVE group I joined and we brainstormed about the options. I knew that no matter how angry I was, I could not just ignore his threats. So I went to our emergency facility and filled out a petition for involuntary commitment.

When I went to the police station to file a warrant to pick up my father, I was still telling myself it was only a threat to scare me into giving him money, but a call was coming over the police radio that an ambulance was taking my father to the hospital for a drug overdose. They pumped his stomach and found a small amount of sleeping pills. It would have been called an unfortunate accident, but the police had my warrant and commitment papers. He really was suicidal!

Soon afterward my support person met with him and told him that there could be no relationship with me until he joined Gamblers Anonymous and started to work with them. I agreed to attend a "family meeting" at the hospital. It was a very difficult and emotional meeting, but when it was over I felt relieved at having told my father, for the first time, what it was like to be his daughter and how much shame I felt about his gambling.

I could never have taken a stand without all of the support I received from TOUGHLOVE and I might still be giving in to my father's demands and fighting with my husband about "lending" money. Or my father might have eventually succeeded in killing himself and I would never have stopped feeling guilty.

In North America six thousand young men and women under the age of twenty-five will take their own lives this year. Cutting across economic lines, from poor inner-city to wealthy suburban, more kids commit suicide each year. As compared to the fifties, young people are several times as likely to commit suicide today.

We have so many guesses about why a person makes this final choice. Does it represent a battle for control by someone feeling helpless? Is it an act of self-hatred? An act of hatred toward others? Self-punishment? Anger turned inward? Perhaps it's a psychotic act, an act of madness. Maybe an act of impulsiveness, a mistake. Or is it a cry for love and understanding, a desperate act of separation? A power play that gets out of hand? For some it may be a permanent way to get out of a horrible family.

We don't know the causes and most of the kids we've talked with or have heard from by letter who have attempted suicide don't know why either.

Dear TOUGHLOVE:

I'm getting married next week. I never thought I'd live to see the day (I'm not kidding). My parents and all the other parents I have from TOUGHLOVE really turned my head around.

I started doing dope when I was twelve and it didn't take long before I became a real party queen. It seemed like fun and I was having a ball. Then it started getting rough. I couldn't handle school, my folks were hassling me, and my older sister really got on my case. I just used their hassling to blame them and keep on partying.

I got busted when I was fifteen for a bunch of robberies and sent to a drug rehab. I had family therapy there and my folks and my older brother and sister really let me have it. I just stayed in my gorilla suit,, but I knew inside that it was me and not them. I went home and almost got back into dope, but it just didn't seem like fun anymore.

I tried to kill myself twice with pills after that, but each time my folks got me to the hospital in time. By now they were in TOUGH-LOVE and the second time this bunch of strangers visited me in the hospital. They laid it out for me. I had to make some decisions. The hospital, these parents, and my folks worked out a place for me to stay. My aunt and uncle in Texas agreed to let me stay with them. I had to work in their store to pay room and board, go to school and attend NA [Narcotics Anonymous] meetings, and promise not to try suicide again.

I felt lost at first. I didn't know what I was doing, but I just kept to my commitments. I got calls from some of the TOUGHLOVE folks back home and after a while we could talk. I began looking forward to hearing from them. Gradually, I started calling home and talking. I had the hardest time with my mom. I don't know, but I think we're too much alike.

Well, anyway, I met my future husband, Allen, at an NA meeting. We started going together and decided to get married when I graduated. The time is almost here. Allen agreed to get married in my hometown. I want to have my family there and the TOUGHLOVE people who helped me. I feel like I'm ending one life and starting another. I'm really glad I got the chance. Thanks.

As parents, we don't normally think about our children and suicide. We don't want to think about it and we're sure it won't happen. Unfortunately, some kids do kill themselves, others attempt to, and still others threaten to. Any of these circumstances terrifies parents. We feel like there's a time bomb ticking and we can't find it, we can only hear it. Parental anxiety and concern mushroom but can find no outlet. And the professional community has not been very successful with potential suicides.

An example is the widely reported story of the homecoming queen of North Salem, New York, High School who hanged herself with a belt a month before graduation. Her boyfriend, under a "suicide watch" by teachers and seeing three psychiatrists, hanged himself with a belt three weeks later.

Mary Giffin, a psychiatrist, and Carol Felsenthal, in their book *A Cry for Help,* state that "Psychiatrists are not a guarantee against suicide. They may ironically be too attuned to suicide to help a suicidal patient. So aware are some psychiatrists of the high risk of suicide in certain patients that they choose not to get involved. They don't want to feel guilty or responsible for a suicide that occurs during treatment, so they may change the subject when a patient mentions suicide or they may evade the issue by prescribing tranquilizers—which not only exacerbate depression, but also often become the suicide weapon."

Hardly a comfort to those parents who look to psychiatrists for help with their suicidal kid. But according to Giffin and Felsenthal, it is understandable because psychologists and psychiatrists are ". . . people who, every day, see the awful damage parents can inflict on their children." If this is the predominant view of parents by professionals, no wonder parents feel blamed.

They go further, at first feigning moderation,

then they really clobber Mom and Dad. "Parents should not be made into the all-purpose whipping boys. Sometimes they have the best intentions—and a suicidal child. But too often those intentions are best for the parents, not the child."

What a heavy burden of guilt to lay on parents. And what an assumption—that they *are causing* their child's suicide. If Giffin and Felsenthal's new book on teenage suicide in any way represents the psychiatric community's point of view, then it clearly highlights an incredible insensitivity to parents and families. The audacity of their attitude is contradicted by the unsuccessful efforts of psychiatrists to prevent suicide. The authors themselves state that "among adolescent suicides, two thirds have undergone psychiatric or psychological counseling. One third have been hospitalized." With such poor results, how can Giffin and Felsenthal defend the psychiatric view while attacking parents for poor results?

TOUGHLOVE, on the other hand, makes the assumption that the parents and the other children in the family need understanding and support in coping with the awesome emotional consequences of their child's suicide or suicide attempt. Guilt and heartache burden them, perhaps for the rest of their lives.

When Martha first came to TOUGHLOVE, she cried and talked a lot. She still cries. Martha came to TOUGHLOVE to help protect her second son, Joseph, who is doing dope. She came after her oldest child, Manuel, killed himself. She is grieving. She came looking for support, but kept kicking herself and others around the block. She said things like "How come I didn't know he was going to kill himself? How come the guidance counselors didn't tell me? What's wrong with me that Manuel couldn't talk to me?" Martha shared her fear and agony that

Joseph would end up dead also. She didn't think she could handle the death of another child.

The folks in the group let her grieve, listened to her, and often cried with her. They got in touch with other people whose children had committed suicide (SOS is an acronym for the organization Survivors of Suicide) and who were able to relate to Martha out of their own personal experience. The TOUGHLOVE parents also called Martha, visited her home, and had her family over to dinner. Their support was a buffer to Martha's self-punishing attitude and to the sense of blame she felt from her brother's family.

One night the parents invited a local suicide prevention specialist to the TOUGHLOVE support group meeting. He discussed the limited amount of insight and control one really has with another human being and shared how helpless and dumb he feels when he fails to dissuade someone from self-destruction. He explained that there's not really much a person can do for someone who is determined to take his or her own life.

Martha continued to come to meetings week after week. One evening a couple asked Martha if she would take their son, Al, who had threatened suicide in the past, for a weekend at her home. They felt her own experience made her the perfect adult to relate to Al. While she was delighted that they trusted her with such an important role, Martha was also scared. He stayed for a weekend and became a friend of the family. Eventually, he talked to Martha about the suicidal thoughts he had had. Martha informed him that his thoughts were normal and that his bad feelings would pass. His parents reported that Al seemed to value her advice and seemed confident that he wouldn't always have his bad feelings. He talked to his parents about how hard Manuel's family had taken his death.

Martha, in the meantime, began to feel more confident. Her kinship with Al helped move her past her grief and toward action with Joseph. She has taken a stand on his behavior and is setting bottom lines each week, confronting him. She knows the risks, but says she will no longer just let things happen. She is going to do all she can to turn him around.

Dealing with death is always difficult for people, but dealing with suicide is especially tough because it carries all kinds of other emotional implications: guilt, blame, anger, and resentment. TOUGHLOVE groups can help a person work his or her way through those awful feelings, toward a healthier state of mind.

Tonia, a widow, joined TOUGHLOVE shortly after her son went into a drug rehab. She became active in the group and invested a great deal of time and effort in explaining TOUGHLOVE to the community. An especially energetic person, she was helpful with other people's kids and brought the staff from her son's rehab to speak to the support group.

Her only child, Peter, was coming home from the rehab. She and Peter, with his counselor's assistance, worked out an aftercare plan for living at home. Tonia set limits and made nonnegotiable demands which included: no substance use, regular school attendance, no sleazy friends, courtesy and respectfulness around the home. Tonia offered to give Peter rides to NA meetings.

The group members who had visited Peter at the rehab went with Tonia to pick him up. He was quiet. His counselor reported that Peter said he was scared and that was normal. The trip home was pleasant. They stopped for dinner, but Peter didn't eat much. When they were alone at home, it was awkward at first, but Tonia let Peter know how glad she was to have him home. Peter said thanks, that it was good to be home, and he went to bed.

In the morning he was up early, as was his habit at the rehab. They had breakfast and planned to go shopping. Tonia asked Peter to make his bed while she washed the dishes. He went upstairs, loaded his hunting rifle, and shot himself. Tonia ran upstairs, saw her son's bloody head, called the hospital, the police, and a nearby group member. Peter died.

Tonia turned her anger on the rehab. "Why didn't you know? Why didn't you warn me? How could you let him come home?" Peter's counselor and the other rehab staff members felt terrible and tried to defend themselves.

The TOUGHLOVE group helped Tonia through the funeral and supported her for months. She kept coming to the group, but she was still angry at the rehab. She would warn other parents about professionals and inpatient units. She wanted to sue the rehab. Group members tried to talk to her about blame and anger and death, but she didn't seem to hear. A lawyer came to speak to the group and Tonia asked for his help in preparing a case.

At this point her friends in the group were so concerned about her that they spoke with her sister and nieces and brother-in-law. They decided to approach the rehab staff. At first defensive, they realized that the TOUGHLOVE parents were not blaming them. Peter's counselor and two others agreed to meet with three TOUGHLOVE group members, Tonia, and members of her family. Everyone knew the meeting was going to be difficult.

The tension preceding the meeting was unbearable. As soon as the rehab staff arrived, Tonia started to scream, "You SOB, you SOB, you killed him, killed him! I hate you! I'll sue you bastards!" She ran across the room and, before anyone could stop her, slapped Peter's counselor across the face. Her brother-in-law restrained her and she collapsed in his arms, sobbing, "I'm sorry. I'm sorry."

The young man she had slapped quietly cried. Everyone cried. Finally, the counselor spoke to Tonia. "I'm so sorry. I wish I had done a better job." And he cried again. The rehab director said, "We share your grief and your guilt. We wish we could have had more control, but we didn't."

All the people in the room talked about their grief and pain and about what they wished they had done differently. Tonia's sister spoke of not being a very good aunt, Uncle Harry felt he could have been more of a father to Peter. They all wished Peter had not died, that they could have another chance, and almost simultaneously they all realized how angry they were at Peter for denying them that chance.

As the meeting quieted, Tonia said she wanted to leave. She thanked the rehab people for coming and thanked her friends and family for helping her face the situation. She goes on with her mourning, still coming to the TOUGHLOVE group now and then. And when she does, she tells her sad story to newcomers, but she tells it without blame.

In TOUGHLOVE we tell folks to take suicide threats seriously and act on them. Even when the potential victim's life is not in jeopardy, it's good when people let the person know that it's an important matter to them and not just pretend nothing happened.

Recently, a young woman at one of our TOUGH-LOVE kids support groups made a "gesture" of suicide. (The kid groups are modeled after the parent support groups and help young people change and maintain changes in their behavior.) Dawn came to the meeting and revealed to a friend that she had just taken ten Tylenol pills.

After checking with her physician, the group's adult adviser found that the pills represented no real health threat (they were not extra-strength pills) as long as the girl drank a lot of water. Nonetheless, the group processed the incident as a serious issue that needed to be resolved.

Dawn told the group that she had just broken up with her boyfriend. She couldn't stand the pain, so she tried to eliminate the hurt by taking Tylenol, the only drug she could find in the house. She said she wanted to feel better and that she wasn't trying to kill herself.

The other kids challenged her. "You know if you had found tranquilizers in your house and taken them, you could be really sick now."

Dawn admitted that the last time she broke up with her boyfriend she was high for a week and that it didn't really take away her pain; in fact, the drugs magnified her bad feelings. Others talked about their own suicidal thoughts and actions.

"When Danny and I broke up, I was high for a week. I could have been killed just crossing the fucking street and then it didn't take away the pain. It just exaggerated my feelings and I felt worse."

"Dawn, next time you feel bad, do what I do: swallow a telephone."

When it came time to set bottom lines, the group members let Dawn know that they felt she had to tell her parents about the incident. She agreed. She also made arrangements for kids to check in on her in the morning, afternoon, and evening during the upcoming week to see how she was feeling. Dawn asked for someone to go home with her to talk to her parents. A support network formed around Dawn to help her through her hard time.

At the following week's meeting, Dawn reported that she'd received a lot of phone calls from members of the group, that she appreciated all the help, that she still felt horrible about her boyfriend, but that she hadn't taken any more drugs. Everyone in the group applauded.

However exaggerated the danger of suicide in this particular incident, the TOUGHLOVE solution not only confronted Dawn's behavior and supported her in making changes, but it gave her a feeling of belonging. Not only did she feel connected to her family or a girlfriend, but to a whole community of people who care about her, giving her access to the experience of others and to viewpoints and alternatives for coping with pain and emotional upset.

Young people need help in sorting out their feelings. They need to distinguish between those feelings that are appropriate to act on and those that are not. How many of us can remember back to those years, coming out of childhood into the heightened awareness of adolescence? It was a struggle just to figure out who we were, what we valued, and how we felt about what was happening to us. Things like getting asked out, feeling ugly, having pimples, saying the right thing in the right place were major life issues and still are. Our sexual feelings were new, uncontrolled, and urgent. Our egos were very vulnerable.

If it was difficult for us, it is difficult now, but in a different way. In the intervening years our culture has changed, authority has been challenged, traditions have been uprooted, and an existential mode has taken their place. Our pursuit of individualism, freedom, and personal pleasure, the popularity of illegal drugs, the advent of the sexual revolution and readily available pornography, the breakdown of age barriers—all contribute to the difficulty of growing up in today's world. The growing suicide rate among young people is an ominous reflection of that difficulty and is a trend that we must confront. TOUGH-LOVE confronts it by saying, "You do not have the choice of killing yourself and we will stop you as best we can," a TOUGHLOVE solution whose bottom line is life itself.

CHAPTER 9:

Incest

Incest, like rape, is violence. Incest usually involves an adult forcing physical adult sexuality on a vulnerable child, using brute strength, emotional pressure, or bribery. Incest leaves an indelible mark on its victims.

I was just eleven years old and feeling real pretty. It was a hot evening. My uncle and his friends were sitting out back partying. My uncle said, "Come here, pretty one, and sit on my lap." I acted sassy and wouldn't go, so I turned my behind to him. He said to his friends, "Now look at that little bitch, will you?"

He said to me, "Come over here. I've got a dollar for you." I wanted the dollar. I wanted ice cream. I was greedy—I sat on his lap like I did a thousand times when I was a kid. This time he had me straddle him and he started pushing against me. In a few minutes he picked me up and took me inside. He pulled down my pants and rubbed all over me. He started pushing inside me, but when I started to cry, he stopped and came all over me. He told me not to say anything to anyone—I was too scared! He gave me five dollars. I never got that much money from anyone.

At least once a week, he'd come around and baby-sit me while my folks were out. He always bought me good presents and gave me money.

Finally, we moved away. That was my first experience at prostituting.

Another young woman wrote us about her family, where incest was an almost nightly occurrence, a way of life. Her father was always after one of his daughters.

My sister Audrey ran away and got all crazy, was in a nuthouse. The old man used to hit too. My other sister married this idiot when she was fifteen and, believe it or not, my mother slept with this jerk. He beats my sister and my sister stands for it. She has two sons and her husband's father is a known child molester. He keeps coming around her kids. No one can believe my family, especially me, the lucky one.

My father tried to come near me once and I hit him over the head with a piece of pipe I slept with.

Everyone was on my case for hurting him. Could you believe it? All of us did terrible in school except me. At least in school I was safe. I left home when I was sixteen to get away from those drunken bums. I've always been sorry that I didn't kill that bastard I call "Father."

When I left home I drank a lot. I started to get into the street life—you know, sex, stealing—

but I met this nice guy who took me to AA and then to Alanon. I still don't trust people, but I'm learning.

Don't think I still don't have sexual hangups because I do. I go to a group called Woman Against Rape. I am really still angry and scared. I feel sorry for my sisters. But they won't do anything different.

I've never been home since I left, probably won't go home till after he's dead.

Then there is the respectable family in which one never expects to find incest. A therapist who works closely with TOUGHLOVE told us about a client of hers who was in treatment at the drug and alcohol rehabilitation center where she works. Rhonda was an attractive woman in her early twenties. Her father was a successful trial lawyer and her mother had an active life doing volunteer work in her community. Rhonda was eight years younger than her brother and ten years younger than her sister. She described her growing up as that of an only child, but always in glowing terms.

Rhonda talked about how caring and loving her father was when she was young, taking her to concerts and ballets. After high school she entered college where she overdosed on heroin in her first semester. She signed herself into the rehab where our therapist friend met her.

In treatment she talked about feeling terrible about her body, her looks, how lonely she felt, how she disliked her father's righteousness and her mother's subservience. But being the "perfect" family, her parents admitted to those characteristics and went into marriage counseling to deal with them. In group therapy people challenged Rhonda about being "too good to be true" and after one such session she packed her bags and left the rehab. She was back a week later after another overdose.

This time Rhonda began telling her therapist about waking up at night as a teenager to find her father fondling her. She would always rebuff him and he would leave. Rhonda never knew how to handle this experience, so the therapist arranged a meeting with Rhonda and her father in which the therapist would speak for Rhonda until she could speak for herself.

Dad, a very pleasant and polite man, came in talking about how much he loved his children, how he treated them all alike, and couldn't understand what had happened. The therapist asked, "Have you made sexual advances to all your children?" At that moment Rhonda jumped up, ran to her father, and smacked him across the face. While he turned crimson she screamed, "I hate you, I hate you! You made me feel filthy and dirty! I loved you and you used me! You ruined it for me with Mom. I could never look her in the eye. I'm so ashamed of my body." She collapsed on the floor, sobbing while her dad kept saying, "I never meant to hurt you. I'm sorry." But as the session continued his response shifted to denial and he mobilized his righteousness. He claimed that he had never done anything and that he was just checking on her at night, while she repeatedly called him a liar.

Rhonda eventually left treatment and went to live with a TOUGHLOVE family. She baby-sat, helped around the house, and soon got a job and paid room and board. She began visiting her mother when her dad wasn't around and developed a real friendship with her, never discussing her father's sexual advances. It was a year before Rhonda would go to family gatherings with her father, with whom she has a cool and formal relationship. She married and has a child of her own. To the outsider, Rhonda's parents are nice and respectable, having successfully raised three fine children. And they have.

As for women who molest their sons, they seem to be fewer in number. But their actions are just as hurtful. Ted, a young man we knew in a residential drug and alcohol treatment center, was powerfully built and covered with scars. His life-style was drugs and dealing, ripping and running. He had spent eleven of his thirty years in prison and was sort of a wild man.

He would repeatedly say things like "What do you think it's like to fuck your mother? You know you're no good, you know you're evil, and you like it. You're powerful and can do anything, you can defy God and nature. Do you know what it's like to get a hard-on for your mom and use it on her?"

Ted used to beat up and rape women. He died in prison during a fight when he was thirty-five.

Brother and sister incest almost always involves blackmail, bribery, and power games. Usually older brothers molest younger sisters and brothers. A couple who had been coming to TOUGHLOVE meetings was shocked when their youngest daughter told them that her eighteen-year-old brother had tried to touch her between her legs. The eleven-year-old daughter thought that he was also molesting her fifteen-year-old sister, the acting-out child who had brought the parents to TOUGHLOVE.

When they confronted the son at a hastily called family meeting, they found out that he was forcibly having intercourse with his younger brother, too. The parents took the whole family for psychiatric help and the oldest boy was admitted to an inpatient unit.

The experience was so painful and humiliating that the parents had trouble coming back to the

TOUGHLOVE group. After missing several meetings, they confided in a group member who urged them to come back to the weekly meetings and to start talking about what had happened. When they did, another couple told them about their own sons' incestuous acts and recommended the counselor they had gone to. The parents were glad they had opened up and were relieved that they had not been condemned. The TOUGHLOVE group continued to provide the kind of understanding and support that helped the parents heal their psychic wounds and go on with the business of life.

In another instance, a sixteen-year-old boy we know was involved in sexual play with his fifteen-year-old sister. The relationship in this situation was not coercive but was mutual.

> We were home alone fooling around and it just happened. I really dug her and she really dug me. For almost a year we played around and did everything but . . . every chance we got. I'm telling you we loved it and each other.
>
> It was like we were each other's teacher. If it wasn't my sister, it would have been great.
>
> But meanwhile I was getting guiltier and guiltier and we kept saying we had to stop. I'd bring home a little amyl nitrate or some Quaaludes and we'd be off again. Finally, my sister was too scared because I wanted to do it and she wouldn't be alone with me and told our mother that I was doing drugs. She also got a boyfriend and I was jealous.
>
> But that's how I started to get treatment for the drug abuse.
>
> Before her wedding a few months ago, I apologized for that year. She told me that it wasn't just me, that she wanted to fool around

too. She guessed that maybe it was easier than holding back or going out and finding someone. I think she was right about it being easier. We didn't have to compete or get out there and meet people.

My folks never knew.

As our culture emerged from the Victorian Age and turned on the light in that dark closet called "sex," we found a lot of things we never expected and some things that didn't belong. Freud told us that there was a taboo on incest and that it only happened in the recesses of the unconscious. We suspect that incest has always been with us, but never talked about openly. Now that we are encouraged to act out and talk out our unconscious, we need to find some cultural structures to deal with incest.

Our personal opinion is that incest is a physically and psychologically abusive act, and as such is not to be tolerated or condoned. We do not feel that legal means are effective because incest is already illegal. Rather, we think that families and communities with open relationships will inhibit the secretiveness that incestuous acts require. A recent television program for younger children informed kids how to recognize inappropriate adult sexual behavior. Although we never imagined such a need before, the fact that a little girl immediately informed her mother about her uncle's actions demonstrates that such programs are necessary for our children's safety.

And we need to confront the drug and alcohol abuse which underlies incest. Our experience indicates that acts of incest are almost always perpetrated by individuals who are drunk or stoned and when their drug and alcohol abuse stops, usually so does the incest. Our TOUGHLOVE groups confront adults who seem to be abusing drugs and alcohol or may be abusing their children, either physically or sexually, offering to support them in getting help for themselves. When this cooperative approach is refused, we recommend that group members inform the appropriate social service agencies. We do not condone abuse in teenagers or adults. While these latter steps are tough to carry out, they rest on our belief that all the children in our communities are the responsibility of all the adults, a philosophy which fosters the openness and caring that inhibits incest.

> When I was a kid, my father used to come to me in bed every Saturday night. I was scared to death and didn't know what to do. I left home when I was seventeen and bummed around. Eventually, I married a gentle, understanding guy and we have two kids.
>
> When my oldest daughter turned fourteen, she started to get into trouble. She skipped school, ran around with guys, and eventually she got busted for drugs.
>
> I started to get nuts and had all kinds of suspicions about my husband. I kept thinking he was abusing our kid and I was being blind like my mom was. He finally dragged me to a TOUGHLOVE group and I began to see that it was my daughter and not my husband I had to worry about. . . . It saved my sanity and my marriage.
>
> My daughter is now in a rehab and my husband and I are back on track. I'm still scared and nutsy at times, but I know I have folks who I can talk to now. Thanks.

TOUGHLOVE can be helpful to families who have discovered incest in their midst, but may also be supportive to parents who experienced it in their own childhood and project that experience on their family. They need the trusting community that TOUGHLOVE groups provide to help them work through their own fear and pain.

CHAPTER 10:

Drugs and Alcohol

Any clinician in this day and age who overlooks and fails to check for drug and alcohol abuse as a primary component of negative teenage behavior is either irresponsible or incompetent. We are not saying that certain young people don't have severe or disturbing psychiatric, psychological, and physical problems. We are sure that a certain percentage does, as in any human population. But we are equally positive that drug and alcohol abuse, for most kids, exacerbates and maintains problems so they cannot be dealt with or resolved. We believe the normal struggle of adolescence is distorted and made pathological by the abuse of drugs.

The single most telling anecdote we can offer to support this point of view is in the form of a teenage boy's journal, sent to us by his mother, which he wrote while locked up in a youth detention center.

"I thought you might find this interesting, especially from the standpoint that of all the 'experts' he's seen only one has said his problem is drugs," wrote she.

"The high school psychologist: 'Not a drug problem. He's a very confused boy.' A psychiatric social worker who had my son in counseling for a year: 'No, not a drug problem. First we treat the underlying cause and then he won't want the drugs.' A history teacher at school: 'No, not a drug problem. He's a very confused boy whose mind is in a chaotic state and running in too many directions. Needs deep intensive therapy.' Psychiatric evaluation at juvenile detention center: 'A lonely boy!' When will the 'experts' *ever* wake up? Wish me luck when he returns."

Here is a story of our times written by an articulate kid while awaiting his juvenile court hearing on charges of burglary:

One day I had just gotten back from summer school and there was Henry and his new friend he had talked about, Tim, sitting up in my tree "platform" (not completed into a "tree house") smoking pot. Now Tim wore a headband, raggy clothes, and an Army jacket. He also was rather obnoxious. He talked rather snobbishly. That was when I started smoking pot heavily. I say heavily because I *had* tried pot before with other friends.

Then my mother had to go to Kansas for a week because my grandmother had a heart attack. It was the first time I was left alone (with my sister, too). That's when I really started smoking heavily. I started, as is the case with most pot smokers, not to care about the way I groomed myself, or my grades, or many things. My chemistry grade dropped to just wanting a passing grade, which I got.

Then the regular school year came around and I started as a sophomore. I did worse, failing grades by the end of the year. In the beginning I was doing badly in all classes, but still passing, which isn't saying much. I was the only sophomore in physics and if I weren't clogging my brain, I would have done much better.

By winter I had cut back enough on pot to get a job, but not to get my grades back up. I also didn't get much skiing in that year, something I love doing; I only skied twice. After winter I started hanging around with another kid, Ronald, and seeing less of Henry.

By spring Ronald had introduced me to new friends who showed me how cutting classes and smoking pot could be fun, so I indulged in that. Yes, we had a really good time smoking pot and laughing. We even started taking pills, smoking pills, snorting crushed pills, such as Valium and Quaaludes, etc. By the end of the year, the only classes I was attending were physics, drivers' ed, and sometimes Latin II.

I forgot to mention that in the first semester I had started gymnastics. In the spring, during which the meets were starting, I quit gymnastics because, as I told the coach, "I can't do a flip-flop." The coach said, "But it took Jim two years to get one. You almost had it now after even a few months." I just mumbled, shook my head, and walked away to go smoke pot.

At the end of the year, we had been planning to run away, the kids from the "shack" (the place we cut school to smoke pot in). For about a month we talked about it, on and off. Then, the week before finals, I was walking along the railroad track and I saw a garage that said DANGER: FLAMMABLE on it. . . . That was the old garage that I broke into and found a pickup truck inside. I said to myself, "This is how we are going to run away." That was on Monday. The next night Chloe, Ronald, Ellen, and I (and one other kid I forgot the name of, whom we dropped off in Chicago) ran away. I was outvoted and we decided to go to Florida instead of California because Chloe's boyfriend was there. Then we drove to Florida, without eating and begging for money, so we could get gas. We made it all the way to Fort Lauderdale, where the truck and all my tools and camping gear and clothes were stolen by a hitchhiker and Chloe was missing. (Ronald had left her at the border of Florida and Georgia.) Ellen and I had my uncle pick us up at the beach by calling my mom, who got in touch with him.

We had pot all the way down there because of what Ronald had bought and what hitchhikers gave us.

After that experience, of which I was found guilty of stealing a car, I quit drugs. I didn't quit for long enough though because I didn't get help for keeping off it.

When you're on drugs heavily and even after you've quit (before it's out of your system), you don't care about yourself, to some degree, and not at all about other people. When I was smoking pot, I used to make my mother cry and slap my sister and punch holes in the wall. I got arrested for breaking curfew, then I stole the dean's walkie-talkie, then stole a pickup truck. Drugs took away my common sense and replaced it with stupidity. I even forged two checks to buy pizza when my mother went out of town because my grandmother had another heart failure.

Then, after I had gone to court and was released on a year of supervision, I decided to quit drugs and attend summer school in which I was getting good grades. Toward the end, though, I got a job fixing and selling telephones and making good money. Making money let me be able to smoke pot again because I started hanging around the same friends as before.

I started taking Valium and tried LSD at the end of the summer, just before starting school.

At school I met people who could get even more potent pot than I had before. I got some LSD and had a "bad trip" in which my whole body got welts and I had asthma. My grades went back down and my clothes reflected my drug use, as they became untidy again. I was associating with the "freak" group and slumped when I sat. The kids I saw before when I wasn't on drugs thought I was crazy and had gone whacko. Their parents didn't want me associating with their kids anymore.

I didn't care about anything anymore. I didn't love anymore. I only had hate. One time, my new friends I met, whom I hung around with at work, and I went to a secret road where we could go to smoke pot. It's a place where the roads are only one car wide and we went through there like a bat out of hell. We were driving about sixty and came to a ninety-degree turn, where we slowed down to thirty and hit a guard rail about as thick as a telephone pole. We broke it in half and the whole front end of the car was smashed in. We went to a house close by and called a friend who picked me up and took me to a game room and restaurant. I called my mother and told her the car had been stolen. That night the police, my mother, me, and a neighbor who drove us went to the scene of the accident. I was still pretty high, so I decided to keep going with the lie. I kept going with the lie even after the insurance company covered it. I finally told my mother two days before writing this. At the same time I told her about what it is like on drugs.

Two days before I quit drugs forever, I got very high and committed a burglary with the person I had been hanging around with, Royce, who had been in and out of four mental institutions. He was arrested for—I assume, since I haven't seen him since—three burglaries and I was arrested for one. I am now in the juvenile detention center writing all this down.

I will tell you what it's like to be on drugs. It's a separation of thought from emotion (except hate) and it's horrid to think of the way I felt when I was on them *or* trying to get off them.

When you're on drugs your emotions are flat or you have hate. I can remember all the times we sat down and said, "Pack another bowl," not thinking that I didn't love anything anymore. When you're deeply into drugs, you don't care about crashing your mother's car or destroying the room your mom let you use by spraypainting the door and hanging motors and crutches from the ceiling and driving holes in the wall. I believed that I was really a "genius" at electronics simply because I could fix a telephone. I'm not a genius by doing that. I wouldn't stick with things. I could rebuild a telephone in seventh grade. But then later on, I dwelled more on becoming socially acceptable, with the wrong crowd.

I stopped learning, blaming it always on the school or the teachers or my father leaving me. I quit drugs for a while, only to go back and get deeper into them than before. I even got a good job fixing and selling telephones for four dollars an hour. There was the time I had taken the most LSD I had ever taken (called a white blotter). It was the ninth (I think) trip I was on. It was also the worst. I have anxiety and LSD tends to intensify my emotions. There, the anxiety I was feeling that day was considerably higher. I went down to the Dr. Who convention and was very disturbed. I even borrowed five dollars from a very respectable girl I knew there. She had to get home on the train and I now assumed that I borrowed the money she was going to use. I still have to pay her back. At that time, I felt guilty, but not enough to reconcile my debt when I had the money soon after. I realize that when I leave here it must be one of the first duties on my list, along with quitting drugs forever. It won't be easy, but I *must* use all the inner strength I have. Oh, God, help me.

This young man's clear focus on the nature of his problem, his recognition that drug and alcohol abuse was the heart of the matter, enabled him to straighten out his life. His mother happily reports that he is attending college.

His journal reveals a bright young man. But his intelligence did not protect him from becoming trapped in behavior patterns he feared and disliked. The sense of getting over on the adults, partying, and living dangerously all create the excitement of the dope world, enhanced by wheeling and dealing. Buying an ounce or a few grams, selling some or using some. Money comes and goes easily, as do the sexual involvements of drug life. This is all heady enough stuff for adults who have theoretically developed some self-control, but for kids it is irresistible.

Kids turn into excitement junkies in a dope world that is stimulating compared to school and families. Doing the dishes or homework, getting up for school, or going to jobs become mundane and boring to dopers. Many kids see through this thin veneer of high times and after a brief flirtation move on with the business of their lives. Other kids become more and more deeply involved. They wear the costume, they adopt the mannerisms and speak the language of their new world. That world is so uniformly stereotypical that kids who live in it behave identically from coast to coast.

Unfortunately, many young people fail to change their behavior because both they and the professionals whom they are seeing fail to recognize the single most important factor in causing and maintaining disruption in young people's lives: drug and alcohol abuse. Clinicians have been trying to treat a preconceived, imagined emotional disorder, rather than deal with that young person's ingestion of substances that alter thoughts, feelings, and behaviors.

The first thing, the *very first* thing any clinician has to look for in *any* young person is the use and abuse of drugs and alcohol. Furthermore, treatment should be based on the discontinuance of the use of these chemicals. If this does not become routine practice, we will continue to miss the boat with a large number of kids who will flounder and perhaps drown in their self-destructive life-styles.

LSD, in the sixties, was seen as an aid in understanding schizophrenic patients. Many professionals at that time recognized the potential of "acid" to stimulate or perhaps exaggerate our potential crazies. Unfortunately, we seem to have forgotten those lessons. So while we deal with childhood and family dynamics, kids will act out their chemical pathology.

All of us have tendencies toward certain quirks and crazies. We might tend toward depression, be a little schizoid at times, maybe manic, maybe volatile. Drug abuse heightens those tendencies, especially in adolescents. A teenager is usually just beginning to get his act together when drugs intervene in unhelpful ways, encouraging him to avoid the realities he needs to learn to face. Drugs, in effect, dramatize adolescent problems. Eventually, the problems magnified by drugs become the basis for treatment and provide the excuses and manipulations that kids use to hang on to their hurtful life-styles.

We encourage TOUGHLOVE parent support groups to evaluate the services of professionals and programs and to patronize those which are tuned into the commonplace occurrence of drug and alcohol abuse, especially in young folks. We particularly urge groups to select clinics and other service centers that include the parents in the evaluation process and respect their input. Too often parents are closed out of the process when they have valuable information to offer. Where parents are placing demands on kids, we suggest that they require the young person to sign a waiver of confidentiality, so that a clinic may not keep the results from them.

Some TOUGHLOVE groups have developed formal evaluation sheets to assess treatment programs. Group members fill out the form for each treatment center in which their youngster has been involved and the information is consolidated and disseminated.

"It is our hope that by gathering as much information as we can, we will see patterns evolve (ineffective program; good program but uncooperative physician; good for one type of behavior but not for another; etc.)," wrote one organizer as she defined her purposes. "In this way we may be able to make more appropriate recommendations to parents considering placement in the future."

We do not, however, encourage TOUGHLOVE groups to get involved in campaigns for antidrug or antiparaphernalia legislation. Certainly individuals will do as they please, but the energy of the organized group is most effectively employed in assisting families already in trouble with kids on drugs. "Stamping out drugs and the illegal drug trade" has been a popular political phrase in recent years, but has been demonstrated to be a long-term, if not an impossible task. TOUGHLOVE accepts the realities of our culture and deals with the immediate problem at hand: how to help families deal with drug and alcohol abuse in acting-out young people (and other family members as well).

The larger issues, of course, remain. How does our society want to deal with widespread drug and alcohol abuse among teenagers and adults? Do we want to continue our second national experiment in Prohibition, which seems to be characterized by the same lawlessness as our attempt to ban alcohol consumption earlier in this century?

We appear to be fighting a losing battle against the drug traffickers. Marijuana is reportedly California's biggest cash crop and the cocaine industry took in more money than the Ford Motor Company last year. But intensified search and seizure efforts aimed at smuggling in Florida and the use of U-2 plane infrared surveillance of remote marijuana fields in California do not stem the flow of illegal dope; it just shifts elsewhere in the country.

Our second attempt at Prohibition is proving to be as unsuccessful as our first. The numbers of people and the amounts of money involved in the drug trade are staggering. Marijuana and cocaine are but two of the products available. Names like speed,

meth, LSD, PCP, hash, heroin, ludes, black beauties
describe the variety available every day to interested
buyers throughout North America. Some are produced by pharmaceutical companies as legal drugs,
but are distributed illegally. Others drugs, like the
"white lightning" or "bathtub gin" of the first Prohibition era, are produced by entrepreneurs at home.
Whatever the source, the illegal drug trade is now a
vast network which involves millions and millions of
otherwise law-abiding citizens who are willing to buy
substances that their government says they can't have.

   We live in a culture that values speeding up,
slowing down, tripping, hallucinating, and living in
other than normal realities. We're not talking about
a few oddballs taking drugs, we're talking about movie
stars and sports heroes, politicians and businessmen.
John Belushi killed himself with drugs, Richard Pryor
set himself on fire with drugs, and John DeLorean
got himself jailed with drugs. Yet the burned-out
druggie on the television show "Taxi" is shown as a
lovable misfit, a comic rather than a tragic figure.
We do not seem to be taking the matter very seriously.

   When a prominent writer was arrested for conspiracy to import and distribute heroin and cocaine,
his lawyer said, "My client is no more than what too
many other people are these days, an abuser of controlled substances." Mr. Cohn was one of fifteen
coconspirators, including a wealthy British earl.

   A Senate aide to New York's Daniel P. Moyni-
han seems to confirm the lawyer's remarks. He was
arrested in the act of buying heroin. He was charged
with possession of a controlled substance and the
commander of the District of Columbia's narcotics
squad emphasized that the twenty-seven-year-old's
needle marks indicated that he was not a newcomer
to the drug.

   The daily newspaper keeps reminding us how

widespread drug abuse has become. A school bus driver was arrested for selling marijuana to students on his route. A Little League team was operating like Fagin's gang in *Oliver Twist:* the coach supplied some of his players with cash and drugs and they and some other kids committed robberies for him, twenty-three in eighteen months.

On the everyday scene, most of us know recreational drug users who are responsible and productive doctors, lawyers, teachers, businesspeople, mechanics, pilots, blue-collar and white-collar workers. People who "turn on" at a party or social evening. People who use drugs in ways that do not seem destructive to themselves or others. They appear able to manage occasional drug use. But we also know other people from the same walks of life whose lives have become unmanageable due to their drug use. Physicians who treat and even operate on patients while under the influence of mind-altering substances. Lawyers who appear in court while high. Teachers who smoke a joint between classes. Assembly line workers who operate dangerous equipment while stoned. Truck drivers who use "speed" regularly to stay awake on the road. People whose drug abuse threatens not only them, but others around them. People who seem willing to sacrifice their physical health, their jobs, and their family in order to continue using.

I'm not writing about a teenager in trouble, but about my husband who is turning into a drunk and a pothead. We have been married three years and we have a little boy one year old.

My husband has a good job with the railroad, but it seems that he's not happy. I don't know. He goes to work stoned and comes home loaded. He doesn't see any problem. I think everyone he works with acts like him, so they all think he's fine. My husband's job is very responsible—a lot of people could be hurt if he nods out!

Also at home he's drunk a lot. Oh, he doesn't get mean or anything. He just falls asleep or is half-conscious. He doesn't go anywhere. I am afraid to leave him alone with our baby. He doesn't feel he needs help. What can I do?

What we've said here about drugs is true of alcohol. Many people can use and enjoy drinking without its interfering and becoming a major part of their life. Many others cannot. This latter group often leaves destruction in its wake: their bodies, their families, wreckage on the highways. All of this is done while using a legally sanctioned drug for recreational purposes.

Drug and alcohol abuse among adults is reflected back in our children's behavior. We have heard of children, still in the early grades of elementary school, using marijuana regularly. Many young people come to terms with their use of drugs and alcohol, often with some difficulty, but they eventually arrange a relatively safe truce. Other young folks watch with dismay and despair as their friends are lost to them, drowning in dangerous waters of their own choosing.

I'm writing about my friend Anne. She is also sixteen. She's not a really close friend anymore. I would like her to be, but she's into drinking, etc., and I'm straight. The new friends she hangs around with are kids into drinking and drugs. She also hangs around with twenty-five-year-old guys and I feel they are really a bad influence on her. She asks for my help sometimes and I don't know how to handle it. I'm not very knowledgeable in drugs and drinking. I think she lies to me sometimes. She's looking for something, but I'm not sure what she wants. I would ask her to my house, but I feel my parents would reject her. I'm afraid she'll try to kill herself or go deep into drinking and drugs. She told me she can't remember sometimes when she drinks. I feel she's into it very much. I don't know what to do for her. Sometimes she gets mad when I say something about her friends. When I do get her to talk, what should I tell her? I'm afraid I'll give her the wrong advice. What should I do? Can you help me and my friend? Is there a TOUGHLOVE group near us?

This girl's feelings are not unlike those of parents, watching their child, like Anne, slipping out of their grasp into a world of booze and dope. Parents write to us, expressing their fears, frustration, and especially their helplessness as their kids enter a world they do not know or understand.

HELP! Saw you on "Donahue." We are awash in a field of pot. Please send information.

Dear Sirs:
I have a fifteen-year-old son who is destroying himself with drugs and alcohol and is making a shambles of our family life. We watched the "Donahue" show this morning and the kids described there were classic examples of what is happening to us—the stealing, lies, rebellion, the whole bit!

Please send me some information on how to discipline my son, George. He is involved with all the wrong people and is using drugs and alcohol. He must be doing something illegal to get his money because he has no source of income. Please send me the help I need to get to help my son before he gets arrested or something even worse.

My sixteen-year-old daughter is beginning to rebel against our rules of the house.

She is a straight-A student, has a part-time job, saved $500, bought her own first car.

She is beginning to stay out till 3:00 A.M., come home drunk, and has had her first speeding ticket. She tells us because she has a job and her own car she feels she answers to nobody but herself. We would like to get help before she really gets into trouble, worse than her or ourselves can handle.

Many parents would like us to help them determine if their child is "on drugs." Like the mother writing the following letter, who senses that things are not going well, but wants some way of knowing for certain.

I saw the "Donahue" show today and related well to what was said. I admire the TOUGH-LOVE program.

Please advise me where I might get in touch with TOUGHLOVE in our area. My son, who will be sixteen in January, seems to be showing first signs . . . minor (if that's possible) dope smoking, cigarettes, change in clothing to headbands, etc., and hours unaccounted for away from home. He is always home when supposed to be and on time, he keeps his room tidy, but we seem to have nothing to talk about. I guess

I'm the biggest problem since I see so many disappointing qualities in him and I am very critical. But I can't even get my own son to get a haircut or participate in family activities (there are just my son, his stepfather of two years, and me). What I don't know is which are the NORMAL changes that come about at this time of life and which are the TELL-TALE SIGNS.

We do not know how to tell people what is normal and what is not. We have heard such symptoms as "extreme moodiness, rebellion against rules, poor school or work performance, appetite swings, changes in sleep patterns, changes in friends, secrecy, isolation" used to describe troubled teens, normal adolescence, lovesickness, and the prelude to suicide. It's hard to tell the difference between normal adolescence and early drug abuse.

The problem with a list of suspected behaviors is that drug abuse shows itself in a series of behaviors or patterns that are connected to a certain drug-induced life-style. Like preppies, druggies often share a certain dress style, language, and values. Early drug use, that may lead to abuse, mimics adolescent behavior. Well-developed drug abuse is easier to see.

One TOUGHLOVE parent support group suggests to concerned parents: go on your gut feeling. Confront your kid and let him know how you feel.

Ask your kid's friends' families about how they see your kid and their own. Tell them you suspect drugs.

Check out your kid's attempts to account for time away from home whenever you are the least bit suspicious.

Check with your kid's teachers to see how he's doing.

If you know your kid is doing dope or drugs or

you see a pattern of change in dress, schoolwork, responsibility around the house, and undesirable friends—come to a TOUGHLOVE group.

HELP! Send me information on how to start a TOUGHLOVE program. I have just this summer went through the shock of finding my fourteen-year-old boy was smoking pot. My third child. Neither of the others were into drugs. I tried to handle it diplomatically. That didn't work. I did all the things people "in the know" say to do. Nothing worked. I prayed day and night. Finally, in desperation, I stumbled onto some TOUGHLOVE without knowing what to call it.

One Sunday morning as I was getting ready for church, I picked up his jacket and some pot cigarettes fell out of his pocket. I went into his room, took him by the ear, and pulled him out of bed. Made him get dressed and dragged him to church. All the time telling him I was doing it because I loved him and did not want to see him ruin his life. I said, "It's your life, but in the name of Jesus I will not let you ruin it. If I have to fight you every minute of the next four years. I would like to have peace in the family, but it is up to you.

"If your grades don't come back up where they belong; if I find any more pot, I'll take you to the police station myself. Only because I love you."

As of this moment it seems to have worked, but I'm watching the situation very closely.

Two nights ago I dreamed a boy came to my house to get help to get off drugs. I saw this stranger stagger into my house and told me he wanted me to help him. I'd like to make that dream come true.

P.S. I read about you in Ann Landers.

And then there are the families who have been on the merry-go-round of drug abuse for some time. They want to get off.

I just heard the "Donahue" program and decided to write. Maybe you can answer some questions for me or help me in some way.

My son, Adam, is now twenty-four years old. He is also serving two years in jail, with maybe more time because he has another court date for possession of PCP, the same charge that he is now in jail for. Right now I hurt so bad that I can't hardly stand it. I blame myself so very much. My son started when he was sixteen years old with a speeding ticket. Then came drinking, drugs, the whole thing. I talked, screamed, cried, slapped, but nothing seems to get through to him. I can't count the times he has been in jail. Of course I couldn't stand him being there, so I would always get him out, also pay for him a lawyer.

Then his father and I put him in a program. But he was only allowed to stay for three months. Then as soon as he got out of there, back into trouble with the police, possession with intent to sell, driving drunk (three times in less than two weeks), back to jail. With the help of my lawyer, I got him in another program. He stayed there a year. This program was supervised very good. After he got out he did so good, was working, clean of drugs, looked better than I had seen my son in years. I felt really good about him.

When he was in the program, we went to family therapy once a week. This meant a round trip of 250 miles. This didn't bother us at all because we love our son and he was doing real good. Like I said before, he was OK. We would visit, write, and, as far as I knew, everything was fine. Then out of the clear blue sky, I get a phone call in September of this year that he is in jail. At that time he also tells me about both charges. I almost went into shock. Well, again, with the help of my older son, we got him out. The lawyer said it would be better if he wasn't brought from jail to court on the first charge. This was on a Friday. He had to go to court on Tuesday. Well, he was sentenced to the two years. I kept asking myself, "Where did I go wrong?" I know one thing. I believe now that if I hadn't been so quick to get him out, maybe things would have been different. I don't really know. Whatever I did, nothing seems to be the answer. I just know that I hurt so bad and I can't cope with him being in jail, so maybe you'll have some answers for me. Dear God, I need help.

I have three other children, two girls and another son, which I never had any serious problems with. My son Adam is my youngest child. There is five years between him and my oldest son. All of the family lavished love on him because he was the baby and spoiled him, but he always returned this love. He is a caring person, wouldn't hurt anything or anybody—just himself. Now the whole family is hurting because of him being in jail.

Some of the inquiries about drug- and alcohol-abusing kids come from close relatives of a family. In one instance an aunt wrote to us about her nephew and enclosed twenty-five dollars for someone from our office to call her sister-in-law about TOUGH-

LOVE. We did, but we never heard further news of the family. In her letter she said:

> My sister-in-law will call me and we will talk up to an hour and a half, things she just has to say to someone to keep her sanity. In a thumbnail sketch, my nephew is in high school, abusive with vulgar language to his mother, plus physical. He has hit her too. No respect shown by Chris to his mother. He drinks—about drugs she is not sure, as she has not determined if his actions when he comes home are from drinks or drugs. But drugs are involved. She has found them and was told he sold them for double the price he bought them. (Their daughter in college is also adopted, but with our niece never a problem. Both were adopted as infants.) Chris's friends are all new in the past year—family does not know them.

> They are a prominent family in their community with keen competition in their business, head many civic organizations in their town, plus active church workers. The minister has talked to Chris, but it has not helped. My brother-in-law, Joe, just reacts as if nothing was wrong, a phase boys go through, never tells Chris what he is doing is wrong, and gives him most anything he wants. Joe especially does not want the FAMILY to know about Chris, plus the TOWN, but we have been in their home on visits and have seen it ourselves.

People, just ordinary people. Our neighbors, our relatives, maybe us. Trying to get a handle on kids who seem determined to "make a better life through chemistry." It's not an easy task and many families and communities are overwhelmed.

But too many folks are struggling with "finding out the cause." Too many professionals are looking for "low self-esteem" or "a broken home" or "confused thinking." Searching for secret, hidden, and internal causes that avoid the obvious: mind-altering substances. Drugs and alcohol particularly affect the behavior of young people who are just defining and developing who they are in the world. Scrutinizing kids who are doing a lot of dope, booze, or other drugs will indicate symptoms of mental illness, even months after they have stopped using. A good friend of ours who works with hospitalized schizophrenics and hospitalized drug and alcohol abusers says that an observer can't tell one ward from the other.

Young drug abusers usually realize that their problems are directly related to their drug use, although they often blame "causes." The author of this letter demonstrates that kind of ambivalence, almost taking responsibility for her abuse, but still citing other factors.

I'm a teenager who is heavily being involved with drugs. I disobey my parents and I have run away, but I do this things because they are too strict with me. I have no curfew. I'm fifteen and not allowed to date. I smoke cigarettes since sixth grade, have been hooked on pot since seventh grade, and I refer to speed as "just candy." I go to school stoned, but my grades are fairly acceptable. I've heard about TOUGHLOVE before and I saw you on "Donahue" and "20/20." I really do need help—I don't want to be a druggie for the rest of my life—if the drugs don't kill me first. I'm straight now because I'm sick and I saw you earlier on "Donahue," so I figured I better write you now before I get wasted again and totaly forget. I used to live in New York. Not the city, the country on Long Island. Then my parents decided to move and that didn't work out so we moved here. It's nice here, but I'd give anything to go back to New York, but my parents say no! I've run away four times. The last time was a month ago and I was away for ten days. It wasn't really anything different because all I did was get drunk and stoned and pop pills. The only difference was that I didn't eat, sleep, or rest for ten days. I was either too stoned, too drunk, or too anything to do anything. I don't have a very good relationship with either my mother or father, so they're more or less like my guardians. Like my landlords. They never like my friends and anything I do is always wrong. I have a six-year-old brother who gets all the attention. I'm more or less the ugly ducking since he came into the family. I wrote this letter because I *want* and *need* help. So please help. I willing to do what you ask. So *please help me*.

When kids are really ready to help themselves, there are usually drug and alcohol abuse services available in their home communities. Most young people get treatment only after they are confronted by their families, but some make that decision on their own.

I wish my parents would have had TOUGH-LOVE when I was a teenager. I broke *all* the rules and nearly destroyed my family. I went from drinking beer at age fourteen to smoking pot to taking speed. I then got into prostitution and later married a junkie. I was lucky. I got tough on myself. I shot up heroin one time to see what it was like and nearly died. I woke up thinking, "How can I do this to myself?" No one else was there to care if I lived or died and it was my decision.

Needless to say, there is a happy ending to a tragic story. My husband and I are still together, straight, and alive. I am in the health care profession. I want to be a part of TOUGHLOVE. I want to give whatever I can to help families and teens. Please tell me where I can find a TOUGHLOVE group in my area. Thank you for your TOUGHLOVE.

Other people use TOUGHLOVE for support after the crisis. Staying straight and living successfully as a family are difficult and parents can get some help from others who know the struggle.

I, for one, was and kind of still am a problem child. I am twenty years old now. And was on cocaine and speed and alcohol. I have been clean for a year and a half this December. I go to AA because I have to and I haven't found an NA meeting yet.

I'm back living with my parents now, I am having a hard time trying to change my attitude. I try and it doesn't satisfy my mother.

So I was wondering if there was any TOUGHLOVE meetings my parents and I could go to around my area. I don't have a car, but my parents do. I'm not aloud to drive it.

Well, thanks for listening and I hope y'all had a nice Christmas.

We have recently started TOUGHLOVE groups for kids, associated with and modeled after TOUGH-LOVE parent support groups, to help kids in the community who are trying to make or maintain changes in their behavior. We know how hard it is to stay straight in a society that is busy getting high. And, as the following sad letter illustrates, when you get straight you have no guarantees that people you know and love will learn from your mistakes.

When I was a kid in the sixties, I lived in South Philly and growing up meant two things on my street. You joined a gang or you used. In the late sixties I was a gang member but as I got into my twenties I wanted out and the way out for me was heroin. Gang members hate drug addicts and that is what I became. After a couple of years into heroin, I went to jail for grand theft and, after doing two years, to a rehab.

It's been an uphill struggle ever since, but I've accomplished a B.A. and I'm getting a masters in counseling. I'm married for the second time. But here's why I'm writing, the sad part.

When I got married two years ago, I took my eleven-year-old son to live with me. We live in the country. I know he has problems from me from before, but he seemed to be doing pretty good—a bad temper, resentments, he tried to go and come as he pleased. But we put our foot down and he improved—slowly.

The last few months he's seemed to regress. Three weeks ago I caught the kid shooting meth. All I can do at first is shake my head, and man, the tears roll down my face and I grab his works and shitcan them and hold this kid, crying. He tells me he's been using since he's ten. Now he's in a treatment center under the care of a child psychologist.

It's going to be a long trip, I think. I thought it was over, even though I know drugs are all

around and other kids are into it, nice middle-
class kids. I can't help thinking, "Blood will tell."
My coworkers tell me that's stupid, but I feel
bad. I thought I made it, but not really if my kid
is messed up. I know my thinking is wrong, but
this is how I feel. I joined TOUGHLOVE last
week.

Drug abuse followed this family into the middle
class. In an earlier era the father would have left
hard drug abuse back on the inner-city streets. Yet
people can still rise above difficult circumstances and
unhealthy family patterns to make a new life for
themselves and those they love.

You talk about parents doing the best they
can. I feel I didn't. I was a bad parent. No,
don't stop me from saying so.

In my family alcoholism goes back as far as
I can remember. My father's grandfather died
in a fight in a bar. My own grandfather had
cirrhosis of the liver and died of it. My mother is
still a heavy drinker and my father left long ago.
As if that's not enough, my aunts are all big
drinkers and our family get-togethers are big
drunk parties. In my family you're not consid-
ered a drunk unless you've been out of work for
ten years or you've died.

Me, I'm sober now. I belong to AA and I've
moved away from my family. That was the hardest thing because although everyone there is a
drinker, there is love there too. I had to give up
a lot. I just celebrated my third year of sobriety
and I still take it "one day at a time."

How did I get sober? For many years I was
working or drinking. I was married three times
and I have one daughter who is fifteen years old

now. So between drinking, working, and marrying, my kid ran the streets a lot.

One night, two years ago, the police call me and tell me my daughter's in the emergency ward of the hospital. My present boyfriend and I are half-loaded, but we dried up quick when we see my kid. Her head is a bloody mess, she's tied down, and she's screaming.

The policeman says she was screaming and banging her head on a brick wall.

They sew her up and she went to a psych unit, where they find out she's been using acid, PCP, meth, and drinking.

They send her to an adolescent drug abuse center and there at the center the counselor and other parents confront me. I am really upset about my kid, my mother is blaming me, even my boyfriend's upset. Both he and I go to AA where I've been ever since and so has he.

But my poor baby doesn't do as well. After six weeks at the center, she starts to hallucinate and is sent back to the psych unit. And at this time she is still in treatment, she is better, but still goes into psychosis. She also has a form of seizures that come out of drinking.

My little girl has been drinking alcohol since the age of seven on a regular basis and I was so drunk and neglectful I didn't notice. So you see I have not done my best and my daughter has suffered because of me. Now I am fighting to continue on my own sober life and to help her have a life of her own.

With God's help, I think we'll make it.

Making it is no easy task. Parents who are trying to stop their kids' drug and alcohol abuse have to change their whole way of relating to their children. They must show a new kind of love.

I began to realize my love was a selfish one. I wanted to do all the giving, to be the good guy, the protector, the home base for all her needs.

It took me many more months and heartache. But after my husband and I learned how to really love, we knew we must make this sacrifice and that she must learn to live in our society with our laws and if we continued to bail her out, she would miss the help it could be to her.

I suppose when she was told what would happen if she messed up "one more time," I was sure she would be OK. But, once again after only three weeks she was gone again. Now the ball was in my court. How could I, the one who had always been there, sign a petition to have her locked up? But I pulled myself together and my husband and I proceeded to do exactly that.

They picked her up and this time she was held until a court date was set. I was not sure if I could love someone this much. I hurt too much. Then I began to realize for the first time, my hurt did not matter, only some help for her did. But I was not sure I was strong enough to pull it off.

Fighting the opposition of my mother and some of her friends, but with the support of my own family, I walked into court three months ago and charged my daughter with grand larceny and incorrigibility! She looked at me through tears as if she could kill me. I felt I would die. Somehow I managed to get through the whole procedure. She was found guilty and sentenced to a correctional school. . . .

We are beginning to develop a new relationship now. She has kicked her drug problem and at last she has started to understand why she has ended up where she is. Every day, in every way, she tells me how much she loves me and how much she thanks me for helping her. I learned how to find where true love lies, the hard way.

As TOUGHLOVE groups spring up around the continent, we receive more and more news of success from parents who see their children through the difficult adjustment to a drug-free life and we are hopeful that the healthy trend continues.

Today is a special anniversary for my family and I wanted to share it with you. One year ago our son was arrested at school for dealing in drugs (he was fourteen). For one year prior to this, he made our life hell and our family was falling apart. The week after his arrest, we joined TOUGHLOVE and it has saved our family.

My husband and I realized that part of the problem was due to the fact that we were not united. The children had come between us and we were blaming each other for our problems.

When he was arrested, the police wanted to make a "deal." If he would become an informant, he would not have charges filed against him. My husband said, "No deals" (and I sided with him for the first time). He insisted that our son be charged with the offense (two counts of felony) and go to court. The courts worked with us, asking for our suggestions. Our son was placed on probation and a number of restrictions were placed on him by the courts.

We made it clear to him that, while we loved

him, we supported the law and if he continued to behave like a criminal, he would be put where criminals belong—and we would do nothing to stop that.

We put it right in his lap. "Whether or not you end up in jail is up to you."

He was sufficiently impressed and began to make new decisions about pot, his friends, spare time, etc. He started making comments like "I could get in trouble again by just being in the wrong place at the wrong time." He was giving it a lot of thought.

Today we have our son back. He has become a responsible, happy member of our family. He is doing well in school, does not use drugs, and is planning for the future.

Several months ago, he said, "I guess TOUGHLOVE really works if it's done right."

When he said that, I knew we must be doing it right.

Keep up the good work. You're right on target. We're still actively involved with our group. And we're eternally grateful for the TOUGH-LOVE support.

Another parent wrote to us about her two daughters, Rita and Lois. Rita, now twenty-one, had moved away from home at eighteen. She started doing a lot of speed in order to work two jobs. She soon found that "The crash is worse than the high and my life was becoming unmanageable."

Lois started smoking pot at twelve "just to go along with the crowd." She transferred from Catholic to public school and started fighting with her folks. She quickly graduated from pot to cocaine, crank, alcohol, and acid. Lois says, "I thought it was great. I thought I was real cool. My attitude really began to get bad. I would go on two-week binges where I would cut school every day. I didn't care. I just wanted to have a good time."

Their parents, Sue and Harold, sent the girls to group counseling for a year, but the problems just got worse and worse, while they felt more helpless. Harold wrote about "sitting on the edge of the bed at night and crying." Finally, they heard about and joined a local TOUGHLOVE group. Harold said, "TOUGHLOVE got me to face the problem. It made me realize if I didn't do something, things would just get worse. You can't allow kids to continue their habit. One night our group helped us work out a plan for Lois. We told her she had to get a drug and alcohol evaluation or live with the Crandalls until she decided what to do. She was not going to be allowed to destroy herself and the rest of our family."

Lois was out on the street for a month, going from one friend's house to another. She now says, "I started hating people and blaming everybody else for my problems. Finally, I became really frightened after blacking out for two days. I got into a rehabilitation center real fast after that." Rita got the same ultimatum and got into treatment soon after her sister.

Rita and Lois now "attribute their getting help to the TOUGHLOVE program." They have become close friends with Helen Crandall from the TOUGH-LOVE home they each stayed at before going to the rehab. They call Helen their second mom. Helen helped them get testing for college and they spend occasional nights and weekends at the Crandalls' home. The Crandall children have in turn "adopted" Sue and Harold.

Another teenager who was in the rehab with Rita and Lois has become friendly with the two TOUGHLOVE families. He says that if he ever found one of his children on drugs, "I would join a parent support group like TOUGHLOVE. I think it's great."

Pat and Dick wrote us about their TOUGHLOVE group. They joined more than two years ago after their son, Robert, was killed in an auto accident along with three other teenagers. All four boys were drunk at the time. Ben, Robert's younger brother, seemed to be following his brother's footsteps when the parents joined TOUGHLOVE out of desperation.

Like many couples, Pat and Dick had the usual pattern of couples under strain and anxiety: the marshmallow and the toughie. Pat was the marshmallow. She tended to be the peacemaker, trying to be reasonable and rational, believing things would get better if only Dick wasn't so damned demanding. Dick was the toughie. He was always after his kids to do the chores, their homework, and believed things would get better if only Pat wouldn't be so damned uninvolved.

Robert's death widened the gap between them, as did Ben's increasingly poor behavior, including school failure, verbal abuse, and sometimes physical abuse of Pat. By the time they came to TOUGH-LOVE, Dick had moved out and they were contemplating divorce. They came to a TOUGHLOVE Weekend Workshop as a last resort. They accepted the message that they had to put aside their differences right now because they both loved Ben and he needed their help. They went back home to their community and started their own TOUGHLOVE group. The following is a letter Pat sent us recently.

We just celebrated the second anniversary of our TOUGHLOVE group. We had seventy parents at the meeting, several teachers, a policeman, probation officers, and some counselors from the shelter. We used Phyllis's tape—

recovery and reconciliation—in the information session and it triggered a lot of memories.

Gwen, whose daughter ran away two months ago, started talking about how badly she felt and Dick and I sat holding hands and crying. Without realizing it, the whole group ended up holding hands and for the first time I really talked about Robert. Another mother whose son was killed in the same accident came over and we just held each other and cried. What a scene. It was all we could do to go on with the meeting.

Well, some good news. Ben graduated last week and he's been offered several academic scholarships. Just think. Two years ago we thought he had oatmeal for brains. He wants to eventually work in the drug and alcohol field to see if he can help kids like himself and Robert.

We've had some other great successes in our group: a fourteen-year-old boy has made a complete turnaround (it took the parents a year of making tough stands and *sticking by them*); we helped a mother to have the courage to place her fifteen-year-old son in a rehab center (she found out he is a near-hard-core addict) and he is currently waiting to go into a halfway house; we helped parents to finally have their sixteen-year-old son arrested (for possessing stolen merchandise) and they are willing to let him pay the consequences for his actions now; and parents who made their fifteen-year-old daughter work at their grocery store for the two days she was suspended from school, instead of just laying around the house watching soaps. (They worked her so hard she came home each day and went straight to bed.)

I've recently experienced how TOUGH-LOVE can work between cities a distance apart.

A daughter of one of our group members was sent to a girls' school 250 miles away. Her mom got the number of the TOUGHLOVE group nearby and these parents visit her once a week. This has allowed her mom (a single woman) to withdraw from her and put the pressure on her kid to admit to and begin working on her problems (drug addiction and alcoholism). Her problems didn't develop overnight and we work with her mom on supporting her during this time.

I've recently been told by my group, my friends, my mother, and my sister that I've changed so much and am much easier to get along with and they like me much more. What a compliment! And it's all thanks to TOUGH-LOVE. I've still got a lot of growing yet to do and I continue to work on "me" every single day.

I am so thankful for TOUGHLOVE and all of you for all of your hard work. I just can't tell you enough—thank you, God bless you all, and I love you.

Each of the letters represents different folks finding their own solutions to the dilemma of drug and alcohol abuse. We do not provide the answers, just the path. The parents use the TOUGHLOVE meetings, structures, and concepts as an operating framework and find their own creative solutions for each individual situation. They have turned their groups into large extended families which actively support each other in times of need and have remade their communities through their cooperative efforts to help one another's children.

CHAPTER 11:

Community

We adults have ushered in the addictive generation and we are addicted to many things. Food. Cigarettes. Drugs. We have support groups for people trying to deal with their addictions: for overeaters trying to diet, for smokers trying to quit, and for drug abusers trying to curb their own particular vice. In some ways we are also addicted to ourselves. We live in a narcissistic era where our culture urges us to pay attention to "me," to indulge our feelings and to do "our own thing," to develop and assert and explore our "selves." We look out for "number one," even if it means busting up a family.

We are the addictive generation, creating an addictive society, and we behave like addicts toward our children. Stanton Peele, in *How Much Is Too Much?*, describes an addictive experience as having the following hallmarks. It eradicates awareness. It hurts other involvements. It lowers self-esteem. It is not pleasurable. It is predictable. All of these descriptors fit the experience that we parents have when our kids get in trouble. As parents, we are so involved with our sons and daughters that we lose perspective. We lose awareness, ignore other involvements, feel a tremendous loss of self-esteem, and get no pleasure from our predictable behavior: repeatedly rescuing our kids from the consequences of their destructiveness.

In TOUGHLOVE, using the support group somewhat like an alcoholic uses Alcoholics Anonymous, we substitute other behavior for our addictive patterns. We get support and encouragement from people who have experienced the same addiction.

What we—as a society—need to do is move through the excessive individuality of the current addictive era to a new cooperative society. We have to achieve a more effective balance between the needs of the individual and the needs of our communities.

TOUGHLOVE emphasizes that kind of involvement and cooperation. People helping themselves and helping each other. The result is synergy: the extra energy achieved by cooperation. When synergy occurs, the whole is greater than the sum of its parts, people are working together as one, and individuals *voluntarily* commit themselves to serving the community. Like athletes, people put aside their differences and act as a team, committed to shared goals.

TOUGHLOVE groups have tried many cooperative projects. In some communities parents have volunteered to help monitor in-school or weekend suspension programs for kids who would otherwise be suspended away from school on school days. Working as unpaid assistants to teachers, they have forged healthy new relationships that make school people feel less isolated and more supported. TOUGHLOVE groups regularly cooperate with government and community agencies to bring effective consequences to bear on a kid in trouble. Juvenile probation, child welfare, the school guidance counselor, the assistant principal, the parents, the TOUGHLOVE support parents, the local police, and the judge work together and implement plans to accomplish changes in a young person's behavior. Kids sense that the community is acting as a whole and that they cannot manipulate the adults who are communicating and cooperating with one another.

But we need to go further. Not just TOUGH-LOVE parents, not just institutions, government agencies, and professionals connected with the problem, but everyone needs to come together to deal with destructive young people in the community. As adults, we have a responsibility for all of the children in the community. We are affected by one another, like it or not, and we can get more of what we all want by focusing less on our differences and more on the common ground we share.

We need to put aside old mass society labels—like "liberal" and "conservative"—and recognize that most of us agree on many things. We almost all oppose incest, we almost all agree that sex at an early age is harmful, we almost all concur that drug and alcohol abuse by teenagers is destructive. But as individuals, we tend to leave the task of dealing with these issues to others, to schools, to the government, to individual parents. We usually don't feel connected enough to our community or to the problem to actually participate in the solution.

How realistic is joint community action? We know that some will dismiss all this talk of community cooperation as pie-eyed optimism. But it's not. It's already happening in many places.

We, the authors, are most familiar with the cooperative developments that have occurred in association with the Community Service Foundation in Bucks County, Pennsylvania. The Foundation began as a private secondary school and counseling program for kids in trouble with the law and eventually worked together with TOUGHLOVE. Many of the parents in nearby local TOUGHLOVE groups became aware of the Foundation's program for teenagers, called "ACTION," and encouraged the development of another school-counseling site in the more populous end of Bucks County, near Philadelphia. But they did more than encourage, they began to raise money.

Although only a few children of TOUGHLOVE parents are ever likely to go to the school, as most of the placements come from Juvenile Probation or Child and Youth Social Services, the TOUGHLOVE groups felt the school would be good for the community and have raised more than seven thousand dollars so far to help make it happen. They have found that others in the community share their concern and have contributed to the effort. The largest newspaper in Bucks County, the *Courier-Times*, announced the plans for the new Community Service Foundation school. Obviously the editor of the newspaper saw this as a significant event.

In a related development, the Community Service Foundation and the Penn Foundation for Mental Health, one of the first community mental health clinics in America, have agreed to jointly operate a daily program for disturbed teenagers living at home, using the same ACTION approach as the existing school/counseling program. The program provides a low-cost alternative to institutionalizing these young people in mental hospitals. The joint program requires a great deal of cooperation and trust, for each organization is going to have to compromise and give up some of its autonomy in order to make the program work. The advantage of this collaboration is that the program will draw on the strengths of the entire community, a synergistic arrangement that gets us past our present destructive, addictive patterns.

Probation officers, group home parents, case-workers, and other professionals who work with troubled teenagers in our county have found that many kids in the school are making dramatic changes in behavior. The best results occur when kids are "cornered" by the adults and told clearly that no one is going to accept their drunkenness, their stealing, their lying, or other outrageous behavior. When everyone collaborates in delivering a strong message, the young person feels that he or she "has to change" and makes good use of the structured support that ACTION provides for that purpose.

Bringing so many people together in cooperative strategies required several years to achieve, as people slowly developed trust and mutual respect. But the Community Service Foundation staff can now rely on well-coordinated support from most probation officers, caseworkers, school officials, parents, and even neighbors near the school. The proprietor of the grocery store across the street has collaborated with the school staff in pressing charges against kids who have shoplifted, so that the kids in the school recognize that there are consequences for stealing. That kind of cooperation allows the school to exist in a community setting, avoids antagonizing local businesses and residents, and uses those people as helpful resources for dealing with troubled young people.

The possibilities for a more cooperative society exist in all aspects of community life, but TOUGH-LOVE is a place to start for those concerned about the large number of kids in trouble today. We all have a stake in the next generation. With cooperation we can accomplish more with less. TOUGHLOVE parent support groups, for instance, have helped thousands of families at no cost to government and at a miniscule financial expense to the families themselves.

We hope to accomplish the same dramatic results with the TOUGHLOVE For Kids support groups. Associated with parent support groups or community institutions like schools or mental health clinics, the TOUGHLOVE For Kids groups help young people make and maintain changes. Kids who have been in drug rehabilitation programs or who are trying to give up a "run-to" life-style need support. They need to associate with other kids who are struggling or have struggled with similar issues. Participation in the support group and association with the adults who act as the group's resource people maximize a kid's chances for success.

The rapid changes in values and traditions challenge us all. We don't know how to cope yet, but we are learning. Therapists deal with their clients differently. TOUGHLOVE parents are demanding that professionals reexamine their attitudes toward adolescents and their families, especially toward parents. The *Family Networker*, a popular publication among family therapists, has carried many articles and letters addressing TOUGHLOVE and the issues that it raises, especially parent-blaming, an attitude all too typical of many professionals. There are psychologists, psychiatrists, counselors, and therapists who will have to learn to talk differently to their clients.

As a society, we are also discussing the issues, on talk shows, in newspaper columns, at community meetings. We are trying to deal with matters like age differentiation and appropriateness. For instance, many states that lowered the legal age for drinking alcoholic beverages a few years ago are reconsidering or have raised the age again. An increase in automobile accidents and deaths due to young drunken drivers has challenged the wisdom of the initial change. Age appropriateness for issues like dating, smoking, or sexual activity concerns us all and we are struggling to redefine our standards and values after the turmoil of recent decades.

We don't need to change our institutions as much as we have to change the way we look at them and use them. We need to free ourselves up and think creatively. Like the parents who asked their local police to wave at their kid whenever they saw him driving. Having been in trouble with his driving before, he now felt that the police were keeping an eye out for him personally, a helpful reminder to stay straight and drive carefully.

We may have to take some risks. Like the school that put aside the legal issue of kids' confidentiality to bring together parents of kids whom they suspected as potential suicides. A psychologist quoted in *USA Today* called their action "hysterical," but we feel that the school acted responsibly, putting its concern for the welfare of the children above any possible legal risks to itself. Similarly, a woman school bus driver in Massachusetts drove her big orange vehicle right to the police station because she was tired of smelling marijuana smoke on the bus. The school administration suspended service to all the kids on the bus because everyone denied knowing who was smoking, despite the uproar from parents who insisted it wasn't their kid and their kid shouldn't have to reveal the smokers' identities. Both the bus driver and the school had the courage to confront the issue, despite the risks.

We must also reexamine the myth of parental control. We persist in the delusion that parents have the ability to make their teenagers do what they want and that when kids don't, it's their parents' fault. Blaming parents gets kids and the rest of us off the hook and avoids the truth: that kids are raised by their community also. Especially as teenagers, young people are influenced by their entire milieu, not just their parents, and factors outside the home become increasingly influential as they grow older. A gentleman in the audience at a recent speaking engagement of ours suddenly grasped what we were trying to express.

"I'm just fascinated by your point," he said. "We're all accountable for each other. I realize as I'm sitting here how many times I have avoided dealing with teenagers in the community who I see doing something wrong. I turn my head and look the other way. But I need to say something or do something instead."

Exactly. We need not become vigilantes, but we need to get involved. Together we will change things. Nobody will do it for us. Welcome aboard. *We* are the solution.

For further information about TOUGHLOVE, send a self-addressed, stamped envelope to:

TOUGHLOVE
P.O. Box 1069
Doylestown, Pennsylvania 18901

ABOUT THE AUTHORS

Phyllis York and **David York** are the founders of TOUGHLOVE. The Yorks' troubles with their own adolescent daughter sparked the TOUGHLOVE program.

Ted Wachtel is the founder of an alternative school and counseling program for troubled teenagers in Bucks County, Pennsylvania. He is married and the father of three children.

Heartwarming Books of Faith and Inspiration

☐ 28229-8 TALKING TO YOUR CHILD
           ABOUT GOD,
           David Heller $3.95

☐ 27484-8 LIFE AFTER LIFE, $4.95
           Raymond Moody

☐ 25669-6 THE HIDING PLACE, $4.50
           Corrie ten Boom

☐ 27375-2 FASCINATING WOMANHOOD, $4.95
           Helen Andelin

☐ 27943-2 BIBLE AS HISTORY,
           Werner Keller $5.95

☐ 26249-1 "WITH GOD ALL THINGS ARE $4.50
           POSSIBLE",
           Life Study Fellowship

☐ 27088-5 MYTHS TO LIVE BY, $5.95
           Joseph Campbell

Buy them at your local bookstore or use this page to order.

HEARTWARMING BOOKS OF FAITH AND INSPIRATION

Charles Swindoll

☐ 27112-1   **LIVING ON THE RAGGED EDGE** $4.99

☐ 27524-0   **HAND ME ANOTHER BRICK** $3.95

☐ 27334-5   **THREE STEPS FORWARD**
                 TWO STEPS BACK $3.95

Robert Schuller

☐ 26458-3   **THE BE (HAPPY) ATTITUDES** $4.95

☐ 26890-2   **BE HAPPY YOU ARE LOVED** $4.50

☐ 24704-2   **TOUGH-MINDED FAITH FOR**
                 TENDER-HEARTED PEOPLE $4.99

☐ 27332-9   **TOUGH TIMES NEVER LAST**
                 BUT TOUGH PEOPLE DO! $4.95

Og Mandino

☐ 27742-1   **CHRIST COMMISSION** $4.50

☐ 26084-7   **GIFT OF ACABAR** $4.50

☐ 27972-6   **THE GREATEST MIRACLE**
                 IN THE WORLD $4.50

☐ 27757-X   **THE GREATEST SALESMAN**
                 IN THE WORLD $4.99

☐ 28038-4   **THE GREATEST SECRET**
                 IN THE WORLD $4.99

☐ 27825-8   **GREATEST SUCCESS IN THE WORLD** $4.99

☐ 28674-9   **A BETTER WAY TO LIVE** $4.50

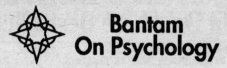

Bantam
On Psychology

☐ 28037-6   **MEN WHO HATE WOMEN &**
THE WOMEN WHO LOVE THEM
Dr. Susan Forward $5.99

☐ 26401-X   **MORE HOPE AND HELP FOR YOUR NERVES**
Claire Weekes $4.50

☐ 27043-5   **THE POWER OF THE SUBCONSCIOUS MIND**
Dr. J. Murphy $4.50

☐ 34367-X   **TEACH ONLY LOVE** Gerald Jampolsky, M.D.
(A Large Format Book) $8.95

ALSO AVAILABLE ON AUDIO CASSETTE

☐ 45142-1   **WHEN AM I GOING TO BE HAPPY? BREAK THE**
EMOTIONAL BAD HABITS THAT KEEP YOU FROM
REACHING YOUR POTENTIAL
Penelope Russianoff, Ph.D $8.95

☐ 45167-7   **TEACH ONLY LOVE** Gerald Jampolsky $8.95

☐ 45218-5   **LIFE IS UNCERTAIN, EAT DESSERT FIRST: Finding**
the Joy You Deserve
Sol Gordon and Harold Brecher $8.95

Buy them at your local bookstore or use this handy page for ordering:

Bantam Books, Dept. ME, 414 East Golf Road, Des Plaines, IL 60016

Please send me the items I have checked above. I am enclosing $ _____
(please add $2.50 to cover postage and handling). Send check or money
order, no cash or C.O.D.s please. (Tape offer good in USA only.)

Mr/Ms _____

Address _____

City/State_____ Zip_____

ME-8/91

Please allow four to six weeks for delivery.
Prices and availability subject to change without notice.

We Deliver!
And So Do These Bestsellers.